SECRET GARDENS OF SANTA FE

SECRET GARDENS OF SANTA FE

SYDNEY LeBLANC *photographs by* CHARLES MANN

RIZZOLI
NEW YORK

First published in the United States of America
in 1997 by
Rizzoli International Publications, Inc.
300 Park Avenue South
New York, NY 10010

Paperback edition printed in 2004
ISBN: 0-8478-2681-3 (PB)

Copyright © 1997 Rizzoli International
Publications, Inc. Text © Sydney LeBlanc.
Photographs © Charles Mann.

Library of Congress Cataloging-in-Publications
    Secret gardens of Santa Fe / Sydney LeBlanc ;
photographs by Charles Mann.
    p.   cm.
    ISBN 0-8478-2034-3 (hc)
    1. Gardens—New Mexico—Santa Fe. 2. Gar-
dens—New Mexico—Santa Fe—Pictorial
works. I. Title.
SB466.U65S275 1997
712'.6'0978956—dc21   97-11858
                    CIP

Designed by Joseph Guglietti

Printed in China

Pages 2-3: Colorful molas *have been strung together to make an eye-catching banner that hangs outside an art gallery on Canyon Road.*

Page 4: A fruit tree blooms in the Santa Fe spring.

Opposite: The first daffodils and tulips of spring look especially vivid in the Matteucci garden, where the old weathered gate, stone wall, and lichen-covered rock convey the property's historic roots.

CONTENTS

*Birdcages and geraniums
enliven the courtyard
wall of the Vandenbark
Garden, also seen on
pages 12-13.*

Preface

The first time I saw Santa Fe stands out in my memory, like the first time I saw Paris. It was the summer of 1978, and in two days I had driven eighteen hours west, across the Texas Panhandle and the New Mexican desert, to visit a friend's new home on Canyon Road. As I approached my destination, the power of the bright light, the vast empty spaces, and the infinite colorations of the desert landscape gradually introduced themselves. Finally, Santa Fe appeared, simple and strong and totally unique in its beauty. The continuity of the adobe architecture, the dusty winding streets, the wonderful food, and the easy-going character of the people make this city like no place else in America. For me, there was also the feeling of elation that coincided with being in Santa Fe. I know now that this feeling comes from venturing too quickly from sea level to an altitude of seven thousand feet. But elation seemed like a normal part of the Santa Fe experience to me.

My subsequent trips confirmed those first favorable impressions of Santa Fe, and I soon came to see the rewards of looking closely as well. This book is the result of my long-standing curiosity about the gardens hidden behind adobe walls. In pursuing the idea for the book, I was fortunate to meet my collaborator, Charles Mann, a Santa Fe garden photographer and plant specialist who shared my conviction that a book on Santa Fe gardens would be an exciting prospect. His stunning photographs and his insights are evident on virtually every page.

The enjoyment of creating this book has been enhanced by the cooperation and assistance of a remarkable group of people. We would like to thank, first and foremost, the garden owners who welcomed us into their private domains and shared their expertise with us: Carol Anthony; Celeste and Armand Bartos; Barbara and Ronald Balser; Elizabeth Berry; Elspeth Bobbs; Dianne and Berry Cash; Linda and James Cohen; Edgar Daniels; Josette and Volker de la Harpe; Nancy Dickenson; Lois Snyderman, Executive Director of The Historic Santa Fe Foundation; Mel Fillini and Ron Robles; James Havard; John Kania; Nedra and Richard Matteucci; Lupe Murchison; Ford Ruthling; Beth and Charles Miller; Clare and Eugene Thaw; Andrew Ungerleider; Tina Rousselot; and Joyce and Van Vandenbark.

We visited over seventy beautiful gardens in and around Santa Fe, and we wish we could have included each one in this book. Many people aided us, and we would like to thank them for their time and their help: Douglas Atwill; the Duchess of Bedford; Laura Carpenter; Cheryl Charles; Catherine Colby; Deborah Dant; Brian Dennehy; Bruce Donnell; Jane Douthitt; Jacqueline Dunnington; Mary and Colonel Edward Gavin; Carolyn Gilliland; Penelope Holme; Kim Johnson; Lynne Laier and Steve Benjamin; Margot and Robert Linton; Thomas Mack; Linda and Stanley Marcus; Ann

Mehaffy; Nancy "Fred" Mims; Viola Montoya; Forrest Moses; Ambassador and Mrs. Frank Ortiz; Nancy Pletka; Ann L. Rolley; Patricia Smith; Dr. Corinne Sze; Mary Ross Taylor; Robert Tobin; Dorothy Victor and Sam Sloan; and Manya Winsted.

The landscape architects and the gardening and design professionals who work in Santa Fe were also generous in sharing their work and their ideas: Rosemari Agostini; Julia Berman of Eden and Wardwell; Donna Bonner; Catherine and Jess Clemens of Clemens & Associates; Stephanie Davis; Maurice Dixon; Cynthia Martinez and Connie Viet of Gardening Angels; Nancy Griego of Corrales Water Gardens; Ben Haggard; Raquel Hughes of Plant Parenthood; David Howard of Chamisa Landscape; Bill Isaacs of Payne's Nursery; Robert Johns in Albuquerque; Faith Okuma of The Design Workshop; Thomas Mack at Sol y Sombra; Stephen Morrell of Contemplative Landscapes in Chester, Connecticut; Fred Palmer; Charles Pearson of Charles Pearson Landscape Design; Deena Perry of Habitat Design; Dana Rice; Martha Schwartz and Kevin Conger of Martha Schwartz, Inc. in Boston; Anita Statler; Linda Sullivan of Fine Gardens; Richard Wilder of Richard Wilder Landscaping; and Julian Wood.

In helping to bring the book from concept to reality, we would like to thank our agent, Sara Jane Freymann, and the graphic designer, Joseph Guglietti. At Rizzoli International Publications in New York, Judith Josephs and Barbara Williams responded with enthusiasm to the idea for a book about the secret gardens of Santa Fe. In publishing the book, we have had the good fortune to work with Solveig Williams, Publisher, whose leadership has greatly benefitted the project. The guiding intelligence of our editor, Barbara Einzig, has proven invaluable many times over, and the production expertise of Elizabeth White, the Associate Publisher, has ensured the quality of the finished result. In addition, the efforts of Molly Morse, Liana Fredley, and Robert Lemstrom-Sheedy are greatly appreciated.

We would also like to thank our families for their interest and support throughout the course of the book.

Sydney LeBlanc

INTRODUCTION

The natural beauty of Santa Fe draws people who feel intensely connected to this high desert land and its ageless architecture. Every turn in the road brings a striking view of distant mountains, a crystal blue sky, and softly curved adobe homes with high-walled courtyards. But these courtyard walls make Santa Fe seem like a city of secrets, with gardens hidden at its heart.

Secluded behind these walls, the gardens are private oases in the desert—tucked discreetly away from the outsider's gaze. Yet these gardens are too exuberant to be contained. Along the dusty, winding streets of the old town and the lanes in the surrounding hills, hints of beautiful gardens abound. There may be lilac branches tumbling over a wall, yellow day lilies by a wooden gate, the scent of piñon in the air, or the sound of water whose source cannot be seen. Just out of sight, the gardens exert a powerful mystery by their very remove. The gardens of Santa Fe naturally fulfill the first principle of successful garden design: they offer the joy of discovery.

Discovering the gardens of Santa Fe is an adventure into another world, one that must be entered into gradually, in distinct stages. At the outer limits, a ring of mountains encircles the city, shielding it and bearing witness to centuries of history. The city's adobe architecture provides another layer of protection: the thick solid walls that insulate inhabitants from the desert heat also turn a blank face to the street. Inside the walls, and through the gates, the gardens await their visitors in private.

The secrecy of the gardens does not arise from the gardeners' desire to keep the beauty under wraps. On the contrary, Santa Fe residents live in a city world-famous for the overwhelming beauty of its natural setting—the brightest light, the bluest sky, the longest horizon, and an expanded range of vision that lets the eye see for almost a hundred miles. In the old town, earthen buildings cluster together, their ancient-looking walls creating a harmonious buff-colored townscape framed by silhouettes of dark mountains in the distance. Streaks of bright color animate this subtle background, with doors and windows painted in reds, blues, greens, and yellows. The Santa Fe River flows through the city, weaving its own tapestry of cool green shade. In the foothills that surround the town, the cloistered city opens up to a vast arid landscape, a magnificent "emptiness" that actually teems with color and life.

As this book reveals, fine gardens thrive behind the adobe walls. One by one, the garden-makers featured here are pursuing personal ideals of how to create beauty in a high desert environment. Clearly, these gardeners are working behind closed doors because the climate demands it. Their garden walls erect a sensible bulwark against the harsh dry land and provide a measure of security and control that makes gardening possible.

Inside the uniformity of the protective walls, it is astonishing to see the diversity the gardeners have created. There are classic Victorian flower gardens practically bursting with romantic bouquets. At the other extreme, there are Japanese Zen gardens, where elegant minimalism inspires calm and contemplation. There are environmentally sensitive "green" gardens, where nature is the starting point, and gardens where architectural structure has provided the basis for the design. Many of the gardens place artworks alongside flowers and trees—and in one instance the garden itself can be considered a work of art.

Despite the diversity, however, these gardens have a strong sense of place, and they share a number of physical characteristics that help make them special and unique. Exotic and beautiful, the gardens of Santa Fe impress us with their brilliant colors, vibrant plants, heady scents, cooling water, and artistic abundance. They appear to have been transported from a distant time, a faraway place, and a culture more romantic than ours. But they are contemporary gardens made for a casual American way of life.

A view into the courtyard of the Bobbs Garden (see page 118), one of the oldest and largest in the city, in the Canyon Road area.

Behind Adobe Walls

Adobe architecture is a godsend for the gardener. It is hard to imagine a more sympathetic style, since the gardens and the old adobe buildings arise from the same basic element of the earth. Adobe construction and its newer stucco lookalike produce thick, smooth walls, typically painted in subtle earth colors. A perfectly neutral canvas, these walls make ideal backdrops for plants. The soft rounded contours of adobe buildings mimic the natural contours of a garden. This closeness to the earth is assisted by local regulations which restrict buildings in the historic district to a single story and in other parts of town to only two stories. The gardens and the buildings are well suited to each other in size and scale.

As lovely as adobe architecture looks with the garden, its biggest advantage may be practical: the traditional walled courtyard shields the garden from the elements. Virtually every adobe home includes at least one walled courtyard, and many have more, fulfilling the overwhelming need of a respite for plants and people alike. Often there is a separate guest house or other outbuilding on the property, multiplying the venues available to the garden. Gardens thus meander: there is not just one garden, but two or three. There is not just one garden gate, but several.

Because the gardens are confined within courtyard walls, they tend to be small, intimate spaces. But what they lack in size they make up in an intensity that borders on flamboyance. Strongly colored flowers look right in the bright desert light, and most gardens are a riot of brazen reds, electric oranges, hot pinks, chromium yellows, and inky deep purples. In the same way that paintings look bolder on white museum walls, the flower colors in Santa Fe gardens look especially dense and rich against the neutral background of an adobe wall. The clarified light of the desert also acts like a lens, and it further exaggerates the color and contrast in the garden. Each leaf and flower clearly stands out, as if the edges were etched or outlined for precise definition.

Robust plants can thrive here, and gardeners rely on hardy cultivars like Maximilian sunflowers, Austrian Copper roses, Persian Yellow roses, and lilacs (of which Santa Fe is the U.S. capital). Hot color and stalwart plants combine to convey a bold first impression.

In these already brilliant settings, plants in decorative containers become exclamation marks. Pots of big red geraniums, a Santa Fe signature, sit beside garden gates like neon lights to point the way. Inside many courtyards, containers exist as movable botanical feasts where plants like agapanthus and bougainvillea can be coaxed to grow in otherwise inhospitable conditions. Wise water use also favors container planting; since the beds hold scant ground water, pots allow gardeners to single out thirsty specimens for special care. But often it is the containers themselves that merit attention. Embellished with Mexican, Spanish, and Native American motifs, planters sometimes outshine their contents. And many pots contain no plants at all—the containers themselves become the focal point and set the style.

Trees also add a distinctive character to the gardens. The native piñon, particularly, sets a rustic tone with its squatty trunk, gnarled branches, and clusters of piney spikes. This kind of pine takes well to pruning, and many gardeners train branches to dip almost to the ground or to stretch out over an adobe wall. In many gardens, the abbreviated piñon is balanced by stands of tall, graceful trees. Birches add both height and lightness, balancing the color in the beds. Aspens can be grown in some places (see discussion of microclimates below), and when

shady spots that are most welcome. Their
leaves turn a lovely yellow-gold in the fall.
Fruit trees also flourish in Santa Fe. Crab
apple, pear, apricot, and nectarine are
among the species that supply bursts of flowers in the spring and fruit in the summer.

Homes with additional *casitas* (little houses)
have increased garden design possibilities.
Extra walls multiply the options for vertical
designs and increase the number of paths
between the structures. Walkways that
disappear between *casitas* evoke a heightened
sense of mystery. As the visitor moves from
garden to garden, there is the pleasant experience of expansion and compression,
proceeding from an open space to a closed
one, and then out into the open again.

The adobe walls that protect a Santa Fe
garden are themselves a source of visual pleasure.
Since adobe is made of mud, the walls are
not straight and level. Their gentle, rounded
corners and catywampus quality have the
appeal of a painting by Vincent van Gogh,
vigorous yet somehow firmly grounded. Rather
than imposing formality, adobe walls have a
natural, planted quality that complements
the organic, tactile garden domain.

The walls that enclose a garden sometimes
seem to expand its boundaries at the same
time. Like the Japanese, who appreciate the
value of "borrowed scenery," Santa Feans
incorporate mountain views into their gardens
whenever possible. As a background to masses
of brilliant flowers, a slice cut out of the
adobe wall behind them may reveal a view
of distant mountains, framed by the cutout
window like a painting.

These walls around the gardens are usually uneven, and the ground underfoot is typically erratic too. The arid terrain is often
rocky, and few of the gardens start out on
level ground. Not surprisingly, many gardeners
take their cue from the contours of the site.
A variation in levels, or distinct terracing,
adds visual interest to the overall plans. A
stroll through the gardens with the most

dramatic terracing yields striking contrasts of
perspective, as views looking up alternate in
rapid succession with views looking down.
These terraced layouts form the basis for
captivating garden design—before the first
plant ever goes into the ground.

Water is life in the West, and its presence
is a source of delight in virtually all Santa Fe
gardens. In artful fountains or naturalistic
ponds, in springs and grottoes, in runnels
and irrigation ditches called *acequias*, water
is always a most honored guest.

As oases in an arid land, Santa Fe gardens
are made to be lived in. The climate is mild
enough that gardeners can be outdoors up to
nine months of the year. A *portale*, or covered
porch, often provides the transition between
home and garden. The *portale* becomes a
rustic outdoor living room, with casual fur-
nishings beneath a roof supported by wooden
columns (exposed rough-cut timbers called
vigas). Halfway between indoors and out, the
portale provides a protected location for con-
tainerized plants, as well as a relaxed vantage
point from which to admire the garden.

Perhaps the most distinguishing feature of
Santa Fe gardens is the presence of art. Art is
a normal fact of life in this city, and it finds a
compatible home in the garden. Since many
gardeners are practicing artists, the art in the
garden is often the garden-maker's own.

The range of artworks that are placed in
garden settings is virtually limitless. Folk art
styles tend to predominate, and gardens
display carved figures of people and animals,
symbolic totems, and art made out of
stamped tin, pressed glass, or other readily
available materials. Contemporary art, and
especially sculpture, holds a place of honor
in the gardens. Large-scale works with a
southwestern flavor are particularly favored.
The near-life-size vignettes of women and
children by Glenna Goodacre and the mighty
bronze eagles, bears, deer, and other figures
created by Dan Ostermiller are among the
most highly prized contemporary statues that
appear in the gardens. Sometimes, however,

*Adobe walls have a
natural, planted
quality that takes well
to embellishments.*

*Clockwise from top
left: a cutout window
with painted wooden
shutters and a wire
shelf for pots of
geraniums at Lupe
Murchison's home;
the late artist Suzanne
Crayson's niche-framed
painted landscape
scene; an old hand-
made door on Camino
del Monte Sol, whose
pious, painted saints
are now faded; a bright
red gate framed by
twisting wisteria on
East DeVargas Street.*

the gardener's intention goes beyond viewing the garden as a setting for art—the entire garden is conceived of as the work of art.

In either instance, the adobe walls offer an ideal bare canvas that can be used to decorative effect. It is not unusual to see the walls painted with colorful murals depicting fanciful southwestern scenes, religious themes, or geometric motifs. The adobe walls also serve as a carrier of outdoor art, such as the Diego Rivera tile mural inset into one garden wall. Statues, plaques, and little shrines are also often mounted on the adobe walls.

A special surprise is the religious art in these gardens, and the way it is used without irony. The city is consecrated "The City of the Holy Faith of Saint Francis of Assisi,"

and its religious underpinning has never faltered. Many of the Spanish decorative traditions are entwined with Roman Catholicism as it was practiced by the devoutly religious early settlers. The practice of personifying religious deities and saints—*santos*—yielded a specific iconography of religious images that appear again and again: the crucified Christ on the cross; the Madonna and Child pieta; Saint Francis, friend of the animals, stretching his open arms toward the birds; and Our Lady of Guadalupe, with roses pressed against her chest. These religious images and the carved wooden *santos*, plain or painted, bring even more "life" to the already lively gardens of Santa Fe.

Nature's colors complement Santa Fe year round: opposite, fall's chromium-leafed hawthorne and red chile ristra *against an askew turquoise door at the Will Schuster house.*

Right, a santo *fills a little shrine on Forest Circle, with a buddlea behind it and gloriosa daisies in front; far right, purple wisteria against a bright red painted window frame on East DeVargas Street.*

Gardens in the Spirit of the Place

The distinctive character of Santa Fe gardens presents an interesting paradox: How can the gardens look so different—in accordance with each garden-maker's personality and style— and yet still bear the unmistakable stamp of Santa Fe?

In part the answer lies deeply rooted in time. The culture of the past is still present here, and it permeates everyday life. The gardens present a coherent reflection of Santa Fe's specific, well-defined culture: its history, its architecture, its multicultural mix, and the independent spirit of its people. Like the city itself, the gardens represent a cultural fusion: an organic adobe background embellished with brightly colored doors and windows. The earthiness of the gardens has been overlaid with bold designs, hot colors, decorative details, and an ambiance that is artistic and sometimes even spiritual. The gardens also capture the old-world romanticism that comprises a large part of Santa Fe's charm—an assuagement of the hustle and bustle that pervades our age.

The gardeners of Santa Fe are working within a cultural continuum that stretches back more than four hundred years and encompasses three distinct strains of influence on modern-day life: the Native American, the Spanish, and the Mexican peoples. Coming into these gardens means not just a breaching of the walls; it is almost like entering a new cultural milieu.

The basic organic sensitivity underlying Santa Fe's culture can be traced to the earliest Native American inhabitants, who appreciated the alliance between human beings and the earth. These ancient pueblo people believed that humans and plants shared a common origin, that we were all conceived underground and sprouted up through the soil to the light. The earthen incubator also provided the earliest building materials. Pueblo peoples—among them the Taos, Hopi, and Zuni

tribes—built their homes of mud balls and strips, in a method known as puddling. Using just raw earth, they stacked the balls and strips into walls. According to Marc Treib in *Sanctuaries of Spanish New Mexico* (Berkeley: University of California Press, 1993), this technique closely resembled the way Pueblo women made pots with rolled coils of clay. With no grass or straw to stiffen the mud, and no wooden framework to support the walls, puddle houses were usually short lived. Mud building gained strength and detail when the Spanish introduced European construction techniques, but the Pueblo approach formed the basis for the adobe architecture ubiquitous in Santa Fe today.

Gardens in the pueblos were utilitarian rather than ornamental: plants were cultivated only for food. Scant horticultural evidence remains from these indigenous plots. The rounded fireplaces (*kivas*) and dome-shaped ovens (*hornos*) that appear in gardens today reflect the enduring Native American culture commingled and integrated with Spanish-introduced structures. Most noticeable, however, are the Native American decorative styles—the colorful geometric designs that decorate the pottery containers, and the stone petroglyphs of ancient figures carved into volcanic rock that have become garden ornaments.

Santa Fe, as its name suggests, has an especially strong Spanish heritage. The Spanish traveled first to Mexico in the early 1500s. They ventured to Santa Fe around 1580, bringing their concepts of gardening with them. These Spanish concepts are rooted in Moorish and Islamic ideals: the garden as a walled enclave that functions as an outdoor room; the presence of water in fountains and pools; a preference for geometrical plans; the use of decorative tilework; and the appeal to all five senses. Since these concepts had been devised in response to the hot, arid climates of Spain

The southwestern spirit infuses the gardens. In the Vandenbark courtyard, geraniums and marigolds contrast with bleached buffalo skulls and adobe walls.

and Northern Africa, they have proved readily adaptable to Santa Fe's high desert environment.

Spanish furniture and decorative arts have greatly influenced local styles. The centuries-old tradition of carved, unpainted wood that the Spaniards introduced still endures in the heavy hand-carved wooden gates, benches, and statues that decorate the homes and gardens.

In horticultural terms, Spanish Catholic missionaries of the 1600s and 1700s were especially instrumental in expanding the range of plants for flowers and food. As educated emissaries traveling between Spain and the missions in and around Santa Fe, they introduced many seeds and plants from Europe, including the first grapes for making wine in the New World.

The many fruit trees in the gardens today are reminiscent of the generosity of Santa Fe's beloved Roman Catholic leader, Archbishop Jean Baptiste Lamy. A native of Auvergne, France, the Archbishop lived here from 1851 until his death in 1888. Archbishop Lamy was an enthusiastic gardener (and the inspiration of Willa Cather's novel, *Death Comes to the Archbishop*). Nothing pleased him more than to share his cherries, strawberries, apples, grapes, and peaches with his friends, and many seedlings were planted from his stock.

The proximity of Mexico has also had a profound effect on the city and its gardens. In the broadest sense, the Mexican heritage accounts for the casual approach to beauty and a *mi casa es su casa* informality. There is a long tradition of handmade arts and crafts that encompasses woven fabrics for blankets and clothing, hand-thrown clay pottery, carved wooden sculptures, doll-making in papier-mâché, and hand-wrought silver-smithing. These traditions are still actively practiced today, and handmade craft items are sold in galleries and by artisans who set up shop on the Plaza downtown.

The Mexican tradition of handicrafts goes hand in hand with the love of hot colors that look so right in the intense light: azalea pinks, bright blues and greens, chromium yellows. As a result, blankets are woven to render ancient geometric patterns in riotous hues, while clay pots often show off the old geometric patterns in brightly colored paints.

The vibrant Latin lifestyle was met and matched by the Anglo immigrants who began arriving after Santa Fe became part of the United States in 1846. For most of its history, the city had developed in isolation as a desert outpost. But the coming of the railroad in 1880 brought waves of settlers from the eastern, southern, and midwestern United States.

American settlers introduced the modern world into the rich cultural mix, along with a strong belief in the rights of the individual. At a time when Americans felt an obligation to fulfill the country's Manifest Destiny of "civilizing" the western states, people were needed here and all comers were welcome. The Wild West held particular appeal to adventurers, and their participation was rewarded with freedom from the censorious cultures that stifled them at home. Rascals, ne'er-do-wells, and miscellaneous misfits moved to town, giving the city a rambunctious frontier air. There were so many such people that special boarding houses, called "remittance houses," sprang up to cater to this distinct population. These rough and ready settlers also established a liberal, independent tradition. The freedom to do as one pleased became an inalienable right.

Creative people, gardeners among them, were also drawn to Santa Fe after 1880, influenced in part by railroad promotions intent on building a lucrative business. As transplants in a new environment, they set about making themselves feel at home. Garden-makers who arrived from the East, South, and Midwest were steeped in the traditions of the Victorian flower gardens that they had always known. Without realizing the terrible harshness of growing conditions, they forged bravely ahead in the only way they knew. Their Victorian gardens—with geometric plans, luxurious borders, and beds tightly packed with old-fashioned flowers like their mothers and grandmothers grew—must have been a constant challenge, marked much more by failure than by success.

Of all the people who emigrated to Santa Fe, artists have played an especially strong role. Their quirky personalities have always fit into the individualistic mix, and the light to paint by seems heaven sent. By the turn of the twentieth century, the city was a well-known artists' colony. A striving for beauty has always been a fundamental impulse toward garden making, and Santa Fe's artistic population sees the pursuit of beauty as a noble goal. The gardens benefit from this artistic atmosphere, and many artists are gardeners as well. For them, the garden can become an outdoor painting studio. And like Monet at Giverny, many artists plant their gardens in order to paint them. The garden becomes another form of art.

Weathered wooden artifacts, remnants of Spain's colonial presence, survive as ornaments in the garden: opposite, an old wagon chassis at Brian Dennehy's.

Top right, a spoked wheel with Dane's Rocket at Deena Perry's; bottom right, the gate to Nedra Matteucci's Fenn Galleries in the Canyon Road area.

A Fragile Paradise

I n Santa Fe, of course, the climate determines the quality of the gardens even more than does the culture or the history of the place. Gardens do not grow easily or willingly here: they have to be trained, the gardeners say, like horses. The pleasure of creating an oasis in the desert is complicated by an awesome challenge: How does one achieve a garden that offers relief from the very environment in which it is forced to grow?

To accomplish their goals, the gardeners have taken the desert up on its challenge. "Please, tell your readers what we start with here," one gardener implores. Nature has dealt them a tricky hand, which they have countered with their own ingenious strategies, based on hard-won experience with the elements.

The basic elements of sun, soil, and water are the same for everyone. But in Santa Fe, every natural element exists at its extreme. At a high desert elevation of 7,000 feet, the days can be torrid, while nights are quite cold. Temperatures can be wildly erratic, rising or falling up to forty degrees in a day. Soils can be heavy, alkaline, and claylike, and therefore slow to drain. Rainfall averages only fifteen inches a year, making water critical. What little water falls from the sky tends to evaporate on contact with the ground, if not before.

Fortunately, there are many blessings to help offset the obstacles. A complex ecology makes it possible to grow an unexpectedly large palette of native and adapted plants. Three great ecological zones—the Great Plains, the Chihuahuan Desert, and the Colorado Plateau—intersect in the area around Santa Fe. Each ecological expanse has a distinctive flora, and Santa Fe's gardens can entertain plants from all of them. It opens up a fascinating variety of choices.

From the Great Plains come buffalo grass, prairie coneflower, liatris, Indian paintbrush, Maximilian sunflower, primrose, purple prairie clover, and poppy mallow. The Chihuahuan Desert ecology extends the horticultural range with rice grass, datura, yucca, California poppy, penstemon (pinifolius and pseudospectabilis), and sand sage. And finally, the Colorado Plateau contributes Gamble's oak, Wood's rose, three-leaf sumac, big sage, blue flax, and scarlet gilia. Wildflower species from all three ecologies also grow in profusion around Santa Fe.

Santa Fe is technically located in the USDA Temperature Hardiness Zone 5 (with average annual minimum temperatures between -20° and -10°). This zone places Santa Fe in a temperature band that stretches as far east as Maine and as far west as Washington state. In addition to tolerating its own zone-rated varieties, Santa Fe gardens can accommodate plants from three, four, or even five hardiness zones. Such wide range is evident in the most popular adapted plants: hollyhocks, day lilies, lilac, roses, iris, tulips, cosmos, lavenders, and blue mist spirea among them.

The wide horticultural range is further enhanced by the presence of microclimates—small pockets with differing temperatures, sun, shade, moisture, or wind. Microclimates result from the intense sunlight at this altitude and latitude. The forceful sun divides the opposite sides of a wall or house into separate ecological worlds. When sun hits the southern or western sides, heat will build up throughout the day, and this warmth will be reflected into the garden. In a superheated spot, only the hardiest plants will survive. Yet at the same time, the warmed walls will retain residual heat well into evening, which may be enough to protect a tender plant on cold nights.

On the northern and eastern sides, the house and garden stay shady and cool during the day, perhaps cool enough to grow hostas, which are favorite bedding plants in northeastern gardens. But these exposures will become frigid at sunset.

Ephemeral flowers, like these white lilies growing next to a private boat house in Tesuque, attest to the gardener's triumph in growing plants for pleasure despite a challenging natural environment.

Given the microclimatic extremes, a garden can actually be hot and cold at the same time. The hot spots tend to be dry as well, where water does not soak in readily. However, little niches, such as those beneath a downspout, may collect run-off and hold sufficient water for moisture-loving plants to make do.

So siting is everything. Every structure on the property—every wall, every tree—effects a microclimate. Each house and garden is unique, a complicated jigsaw puzzle where the pieces do not all necessarily fit. The gardener is challenged to interpret and exploit his or her particular microclimates to best advantage. By careful experimentation, which entails a certain amount of profit and loss, the gardener learns to work within the microclimatic confines of the site. If the plant is successfully matched to the microclimate, it will thrive.

Finally, the wide range of plant possibilities reflects three distinct growing seasons. Spring begins in March with a cheerful show of bulbs, when tulips and crocus pop up—as often as not through a lingering snow. High summer arrives in late May, when the lilac, iris, and wisteria come into full flower. Come July, the perennials bloom, and the gardens are flush with flowers, including roses, delphiniums, day lilies, daisies, hollyhocks, and lavenders. This is a magical time of year, with abundant display that lasts to late August. In September, some roses will bloom again. Fall unfurls a scenic backdrop across the land. The hills and valleys that surround the city become streaked with the yellows of chamisa and snakeweed, the hues of purple aster, and the reds of Virginia creeper and crimson chiles. Trees play a spectacular role in the color season, as the leaves on cottonwoods and aspens go yellow and gold. The gardens rest in winter, but this off-season has its own charm. In many gardens the structural foliage takes on an architectural appearance in the snow, and in the city the colorful painted doors and windows gain in contrast with the blankets of white.

At her own home, landscape designer Tina Rousselot devised a grid of square beds for her garden, which includes roses, delphiniums, day lilies, daisies, hollyhocks, and lavenders. Individual plots simplify adding or removing specific plants.

How Will the Gardens Grow?

For most of its colorful history, Santa Fe has existed as an isolated outpost in the desert. But like an attractive port city it has flourished nonetheless. Increasing numbers of residents have been drawn to the quality of its light, the beauty of its landscape, and its easy indoor-outdoor way of life.

In the 1990s, the city has started to become a victim of its own success—the limits of growth are beginning to loom. With a burgeoning population, water consumption is rising exponentially, while the water supply enjoys no such expansion. Increasingly, it is the availability of this precious resource that will define quality of life for residents and their gardens in years to come.

Environmental activists began voicing these concerns in the late 1970s. By 1996, when a crippling drought forced water rationing, the need to conserve water had become apparent to almost everyone. As might be expected given Santa Fe's individualistic culture, however, there are angry protesters who consider unhampered water use their birthright.

But choices will have to be made, and they will fall especially hard on the gardeners. No one enjoys the prospect of having to sacrifice a beautiful garden for the equally worthy goal of water conservation.

In part the solution lies in the mind of the gardener—in a new definition of what constitutes beauty in the garden. This shift is beginning to occur, albeit gradually. The concept of xeriscape gardening, which advocates using native plants to husband limited resources, is helping point the way toward a new era. Native plants, once thought of as "weeds," are gaining favor because they are beautiful specimens as well as reliable survivors. Chamisa, a ubiquitous roadside shrub with ethereal, pale green leaves, turns out to look quite fine in the garden. The spiky yucca lends a strong structural presence in the midst of softer flowers and shrubs. Grasses, too, can be ornamental. Indian rice grass, for example, has lovely arching blades that seem to burst out spontaneously in a garden setting. Wildflowers and flowering natives—including penstemon, Santa Fe phlox, black-eyed Susans, prairie coneflowers, wild aster, goldenrod, and blue sageplants—are coming into their own as desirable candidates for the garden as well as the landscape.

Most home gardeners are taking an incremental approach to xeriscape designs, introducing a careful selection of native plants into a traditional mix of lilacs, roses, day lilies, hollyhocks, and iris. This evolution continues the trial and error process that has always intrigued and frustrated the Santa Fe gardener.

Beyond xeriscape gardening, Santa Fe gardeners are also experimenting with the concept of permaculture. A revival of ancient agricultural principles (the term is a contraction of permanent and agriculture), permaculture calls for companion planting that mimics the complexity of nature. Plants are grouped according to their needs, with each supplying the other, in the self-sustaining combinations that have evolved in nature. By utilizing the mutually beneficial characteristics of plants, permaculture begins to restore natural ecosystems. This method conserves water by focusing on drought-resistant plants. Furthermore, the vegetation collects moisture that would have evaporated on barren land. As an added benefit, successful permaculture planting fosters an increase in wildlife, as birds, butterflies, bees, and other creatures regain their place in a harmonious plant community.

As the twentieth century comes to a close, Santa Fe gardens seem poised to evolve with the diversity that has been their hallmark. Whether the gardens are elaborate or restrained, the garden-makers will continue their personal, delicate dance with the desert. Like gardeners everywhere, they are tirelessly optimistic. Whatever happens, these gardeners say, "there's always next year."

Wild natural beauty: claret cup cactus and native grasses emerge on a rocky hill in the desert at Cabezon, with Cerro Pelon in the distance.

Gardening by Tradition

The cherished favorites—plants and gardening ideas that stand the test of time—are the basis of gardening traditions everywhere. In Santa Fe, these traditions are a rich concoction that weaves Native American, Spanish, Moorish, and Mexican influences. Vivid colors, lush stands of old-fashioned flowers, hand-thrown pottery containers, tiered fountains, and sculptures depicting religious or southwestern themes: these are among the defining elements of Santa Fe's traditional gardens.

Today's time-honored garden designs begin with this exotic cultural mix, which is insinuated into the English styles that were popular across the United States in the late nineteenth century. At that time, new residents arrived from the East, the South, and the Midwest, and they brought their Victorian garden ideals with them. In Santa Fe, the English model has evolved into gardens that are formally sited, with linear walkways and paths, and a sharp delineation between the lawn and the garden. Beds and borders are also clearly defined. Within the beds, plants occupy traditional positions: tall ones in back, shorter ones in front, and borders around all the edges. The plantings are also thoughtfully massed by type or by color to create dramatic specific effects.

A delightful floral profusion characterizes the traditional garden. Endearing classics, such as hollyhocks, roses, peonies, iris, and delphiniums, have become standards. Popularized by the sophisticated Victorian-era arrivals, these flowers have proven staying power. Their blooms develop intense color thanks to Santa Fe's cool nights, and this super-saturated color looks fantastic against the blank background of the adobe walls. Fortunately for the garden traditionalist, the flowers that look best are also the most likely to succeed in this climate.

The Garden
at El Zaguan
(see page 36).

AN OPEN SECRET

The Garden at El Zaguan

While Santa Fe home gardeners and professional landscape designers are venturing into new drought-resistant practices, traditional gardens continue to thrive. One of Santa Fe's oldest and most romantic horticultural treasures, The Garden at El Zaguan, was re-created by its present owner, the Historic Santa Fe Foundation. Under the direction of Stephanie Davis, the foundation has brought back the Victorian garden plan and lush bouquets of old-fashioned flowers that were popular at the turn of the century. This Canyon Road icon is one of the few gardens visible to passersby. Because of its visibility, its longevity, and its beauty, it remains an influential component of the city's gardening past, present, and future.

It is a surprising sight, appearing in the midst of the adobe art galleries that line both sides of Canyon Road. Its white picket fence and two enormous horse chestnut trees sit flush with the sidewalk, framing a picturesque view of an enchanting Victorian cottage garden down below. From the vantage point of people passing by, the garden seems to be warmly beckoning. Happily, the invitation is genuine, for the garden is open to the public every day except Sunday.

In other words, this garden is no secret. Unlike virtually all the others in Santa Fe, The Garden at El Zaguan does not bloom in isolation behind adobe walls. It is meant to be found, seen, and enjoyed by everyone. "The garden is not a secret garden in the sense of being hidden or private, although it certainly feels like a secret garden when you are inside," says Davis. The secret of this garden is its story.

It was during the early 1990s that Stephanie Davis planted the colorful flower garden. But this fresh planting belies the antiquity of the garden's origins in the 1800s. It has become a local treasure, a living reminder of Santa Fe's fateful transition from a rugged frontier town to a beacon of cultural sophistication.

"Most people who visit have no idea that these beautiful pink peonies are a hundred years old," says Davis, describing two thick-trunked bushes reputedly imported from China via Mexico. A large tamarisk tree (salt cedar) in the far corner is another centenarian; the two horse chestnut trees are decades older; and the honeysuckle has been there so long its lovely twisted shape seems as permanent as sculpture.

A crisscross plan helps organize El Zaguan's colorful cornucopia of blue delphinium, white shasta daisies, blue catnip, and yellow heliopsis.

The Garden at El Zaguan may be a historical garden, but this "history" sometimes mixes fact and mythology. We know that in 1854 a Santa Fe trader, James Johnson, bought a small adobe house here. As his business and family grew, he added many rooms and a breezeway (*zaguan*), creating one of the grandest homes of the day. The El Zaguan house and garden complex is named for this long, dim breezeway, which culminates in a burst of light and the colors of the garden.

Around 1890, the Johnson family shared their home with Adolph Bandelier, a famed Swiss ethnologist researching New Mexican Indians. Bandelier was an avid gardener, and legend credits him with designing the gardens around 1892, but Jesusita Johnson was probably the creator.

Given the garden's turn-of-the-century origins, it is no coincidence that Stephanie Davis decided to make a Victorian garden on this spot. Her goal was to re-create a beloved remnant of Santa Fe's past into a garden that would be fresh and new in its floral delights. "I kept the original Victorian design—the two rectangular beds divided by the intriguing crisscross paths—and I selected flowers that were popular in the 1890s that also do well in our climate. It was important to maintain the air of antiquity, although I was also mindful of later owners who planted many flowers, like the beauty bush and the snowball bush, that were not Victorian but added charm to the garden. The fern leaf peonies were popular in the thirties and forties, and calendulas in the fifties. These plants are part of the history too."

The ephemeral existence of a garden makes it extremely difficult to achieve total historical authenticity. Fortunately, Davis discovered the original crisscross paths buried beneath garden debris. "As for the flowers, all I had to go on were some old photos that showed daisies, nasturtiums, and tall irises. There was nothing about the colors." She had to search libraries for the knowledge that would assist her in establishing color sequences in keeping with Victorian preferences, as well as the names that flowers in Victorian gardens go by today.

Working within the structure of the geometric outline, Davis devised the new plantings. Pale pinks and lavenders—peonies and roses among them—fill the beds near the house, shading to deeper colors—delphiniums, snapdragons, lupines, and lavender—toward the back. Hotter colors appear in the rear plot. Yellow flowers like columbine, anthemis, daffodils, violas, buttercups, and calendulas are balanced by strong reds, including monarda and heliopsis and red-hot poker. In the middle beds are the beautiful blues of campanula, delphiniums, forget-me-nots, salvia, and scabiosa. White flowers—such as white daisies and lily-of-the-valley—planted throughout the garden lend lightness and continuity.

Although Victorian styles seem quaint to us today, Santa Fe, then as now, was home to a sophisticated elite. "People stayed in contact with the big eastern cities, and it shows in the garden," notes Davis. The delphiniums, bluebells, and even petunias, dianthus, and alyssum, betray the eastern influence upon Santa Fe. "There's a kind of magic in the air when you re-create a garden like this one. The garden was so old, and so many people had worked on it, I somehow felt their spirits working right alongside me. The presence of the past has been retained in the El Zaguan house and in its garden. I think the re-created garden, especially, captures that wonderful mix of southwestern style and eastern eclecticism that makes Santa Fe so interesting."

East meets West at El Zaguan: a native salt cedar tree shades the picket fence and Territorial-style windows.

Opposite, clockwise from top left: a hundred-year-old peony; sunny yellow heliopsis; peonies and viburnum in full spring bloom; rarely grown hostas in Santa Fe.

At right, asters and delphiniums are among El Zaguan's old-fashioned flowers in rich colors.

Opposite, The Garden at El Zaguan becomes subdued at summer's end.

At right, Victorian-era garden paths were uncovered and restored. In planning color sequences, the garden's re-creators searched antique garden books for colors favored by turn-of-the-century gardeners.

FLOWERS AND STONES

The Kania Garden

I n his private life John Kania is a collector of classic lilies, day lilies, and daffodils. In his work life, as owner of an ethnographic gallery on Canyon Road, he purveys fine sculptures and crafts. These two collecting passions might first seem to spring from opposing impulses: the new versus the old; the hard versus the soft; the common versus the rare. But in his garden it all comes together. Kania combines carefully chosen flowers with evocative old stoneworks to create an unusual aura: an ancient southwestern garden with a modern floral array.

Inspired by a love of Mexican gardens, Kania has spent fifteen years making his hillside match his ideal—although the harsh Santa Fe climate doesn't let him go as far as he would like. On frequent buying trips to Mexico for the gallery, he has gained exceptional access to quality pieces that only a dealer could find. The treasures he brings back—the Indian grinding stones called *metates*, architectural relics, low stone sculptures, and inscribed stone fragments—look right at home in the garden.

Perhaps without even realizing it, by placing these ethnographic works in his garden in a subtle way, Kania has made a garden of discovery. Many collectors would stand such exotica on pedestals. Instead, he has chosen to tuck them away among the plants and flower pots, usually at ground level. The effect is better for being uncalculated. Over the years, the garden has taken many turns, evolving into three main areas.

A large courtyard inside the front gates is anchored by a three-tiered Mexican fountain, pavement of red brick, and a wealth of blooming plants in containers. A cactus garden occupies the middle ground on the hillside. It has so many terrace levels that, as Kania observes, "it looks like a Mayan temple in winter." At the rear of the long, narrow property, at the highest point, he has installed a large, deep pool, filling it with water lilies, cattails, water iris, water ivy, and many other plants that keep the pond naturally healthy. The trees around the property, mostly Siberian elms, make a cool covering overall. "With the harshness of the sun on this hillside, and the poor quality of the soil here, it is the trees that make the garden possible," Kania explains.

"People don't realize how hard it is to grow anything in Santa Fe," he emphasizes, on a day when the garden is in full summer bloom. "This is the reason I like to plant in containers. Years ago, when I couldn't get day lilies to bloom in the ground, I started them in pots until they became large enough to transplant. But I never did. They're still in containers— and I have added many more."

Now the classic lilies, day lilies, and daffodils that John Kania loves so much have become focal points of the garden. You can see them wherever you go. Nestled among these flowers are the less obvious but equally important attractions—the ethnographic stones and fragments that appear mysteriously in the garden as almost-buried treasures.

Updating southwestern tradition, John Kania chooses native plants such as chamisa and yucca, combining them with old Indian grinding stones and terra-cotta jugs that recall the area's history.

At left, the focal point of Kania's front court-yard is a three-tiered Mexican fountain surrounded by pots of petunias, marigolds, and day lilies.

At right, his prized day lilies are highlights of this container garden around the fountain.

FLOWERS AND STONES

At left, simple stone vessels cluster at ground level beneath a stand of bedded lilies.

Opposite, a desert garden still life features poppies, cholla cactus, a terra-cotta pot, a bleached skull, and an old wagon wheel.

Fragile-looking flowers and raw stone artifacts create poignant appeal: at right, tiny red tulips with lichen-covered rock and a metate, *the ancient Indian mortar and pestle.*

Opposite page, clockwise from top left: petunias swell over a sedate metate; *an olla lies in a bed of prickly pear cactus; day lilies and a fleabane flank a* metate; *potted agave and specimen cactus set off yet another* metate *and a petroglyph.*

THE GARDEN'S THE THING

The Daniels Garden

E dgar Daniels came to Santa Fe after a career on stage and screen. So perhaps it should come as no surprise that his garden has a theatrical allure. Like a performance in five acres, the garden plays out a range of horticultural experiences. By turns it is bombastic, colorful, soothing, thoughtful, playful, and inspirational.

Yet the stage was quite bare when Daniels bought the property in the late 1980s. "It looked like nothing," he insists, surveying the fullness of bloom on a beautiful July morning. "The whole thing went right down into the arroyo."

This is one of the most ambitious gardens in Santa Fe, and it is clearly built for exquisite entertaining. You can almost hear the gaiety of a summer night as guests mingle with cocktails before an evening at the opera. Near the public areas of the house, open terraces are enlivened with highly concentrated flower power—with the mountains providing a scenic backdrop. Plants around the house and terraces are tightly massed in beds or in close-set containers. Blazing reds, pinks, golds, and yellows, these flowers can hold their own any day, or even on a party night. A garden on the private side of the house, on the other hand, acts as an island of repose, with sculptures of gentle deer amid soft blues and violets.

As the gardens glide away from the house, down the old arroyo, they take on a different character. The extreme cultivation of the upper terrace stops at a low adobe wall. On the other side of the wall, the lower tier of the garden is much more relaxed. There is considerable ground to be covered, and the plantings resemble an exuberant meadow. Terracing tames the arroyo's slide, and a small stream has been reclaimed. Stone steps set in gravel paths wind down the hill, leading to numerous niches along the way.

Some appear to have been made for their sculptures; a work by Glenna Goodacre and a bear by Dan Ostermiller are just two of many works on the property (see page 57). Other niches are furnished with benches or chairs set among the flowers.

In the layout of the garden, the sculpture came first. At the back of the house, the sculptures are larger than life; they are placed as sentinels, announcing specific transition points into the gardens. Out in the arroyo, the sculptures become destinations worth walking to see.

Trees also ranked high on the agenda. "It was important to me to bring trees to the house. We started by planting several fruit trees, and some friends gave me the apricot trees as a gift." In just a few years, the trees have matured to provide views, shade, and structure, not to mention many wonderful fruits.

"I strove for a diverse look, not just a Santa Fe look," Daniels explains. "And I wanted the garden to look good from inside the house." But like every Santa Fe gardener, no matter what "look" was desired, the first obstacle was poor soil. A great deal of dirt had to be hauled in before any planting could begin. When planting time finally came, it

A high terrace has the sweep of an open-air stage, tightly planted with masses of Sweet William and lupines. Its curving wall recapitulates the curving horizon.

happened to coincide with a prescheduled party time. "I selected the plants and I told my gardeners to put them in tight. I wanted the garden to look good for a party I was hosting at the house—that night!"

The garden has looked good ever since. The thousands of flowers that spill over the pots and paths are spectacular to see. Massed in beds, they make lavish displays of poppies and cosmos. Lined up in containers—such as the terra-cotta pots filled with hot pink geraniums around the fountain along the back terrace wall—they define open areas with their repetitive rhythms.

It is interesting to learn that the gate leading to the garden is truly a work of art, aptly entitled "The Tree of Knowledge." This artistic portal depicts a rather shy-looking snake coiled around a sheaf of curved iron branches with a copper apple suspended between the twigs.

In his personal Eden, Daniels is not resting on his laurels. He is planning an encore. Daniels recently acquired the property behind his on which to build a new guest house, and, naturally, to create an even larger stage for his remarkable garden.

At left, in the lower garden, a delicate path banked with phlox and marigolds leads to a secluded sitting area.

At right, a walk into the lower garden begins with a breathtaking view of the Sangre de Cristo Mountains in the distance.

The "Tree of Knowledge" gate, a work in iron and copper by artist Enrique Vega of Apex, North Carolina, marks the entrance to the Daniels Garden.

Opposite page, clockwise from top left, prominent pieces by Santa Fe artists include: a bronze deer, "The Bonding," by Dan Ostermiller; "Ya-ta-hey" ("Hello"), a Glenna Goodacre bronze near the front door; two works by Dan Ostermiller: "Daydreamer," a crouching bronze bear; and a soaring bronze eagle, "American Gold."

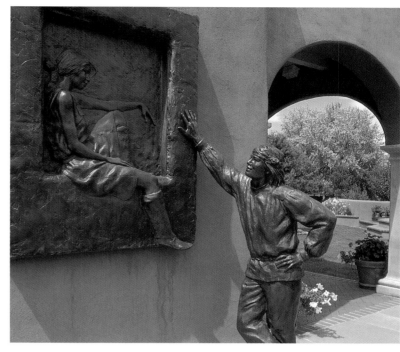

At left, a sweep of gloriosa daisies and yarrow disappears into mugho pines in the lower garden.

At right, black-eyed Susans surround a lichen-covered stone.

A CLASSIC POSE

The de la Harpe Garden

Josette and Volker de la Harpe live in a seventy-year-old pueblo-style adobe home on a picturesque lane near Canyon Road. The enclave neighborhood is a perfect vignette of Santa Fe's elegant East Side, where the rough-hewn history of a frontier town has been tamed to cultivated refinement over the years. Lilacs, the signature plant of the old East Side, line the short, dusty street, almost hiding the adobe walls and houses when they bloom in the spring. Fortunately, the passage of time has not obscured the original garden design. It is a classic.

Like the turn-of-the-century garden at El Zaguan, the de la Harpe garden picks up the strands of Santa Fe's horticultural history and old-fashioned gardening ideals—a "proper" garden, as defined by the sophisticated settlers of Victorian times. It has evolved as a mix of Santa Fe, English, and Spanish traditions. Paths radiating out from a central point form triangular beds that brim over with colorful perennials and heirloom roses. It's an elegant, romantic style that suits Josette de la Harpe perfectly. She plans the garden, plants it, and maintains it. Her husband, Volker, a fine woodworker who carves doors and furniture, has his separate preserve—an eye-catching oasis in front of his studio on Canyon Road.

Josette de la Harpe is an artist as well as a gardener. She has managed to satisfy her two favorite pursuits all year round. "I am out there gardening in the warm months, and I paint the garden when it's cold," she explains. She has also planned the garden with an eye to cut flowers, those that will make the most beautiful bouquets for the house or presents for friends. "I don't go for that solid-mass-of-marigolds idea," she says. "I like to mix it all up. I have found the key to success of my method is having lots of white, and weaving it in. Then you can add all the color you want."

The traditional garden fills an enclosed courtyard flanking their "winter house," which the couple bought in the 1960s. About ten years later they acquired the adjacent vacant lot. On this property they built the "summer house" and its deep portal overlooking the pool. "We move into the summer house when warm weather comes," she explains. "We don't have a mountain cabin for getaways, so this is really our vacation."

While the original garden is steeped in nostalgia, the "new" one is much more contemporary. Its big dramatic gesture focuses on the swimming pool. Josette de la Harpe has surrounded the long, narrow pool with pots of agapanthus. A wildflower meadow has naturalized outside the adobe walls of the summer house. Dwarf fruit trees planted here—apples, peach, nectarine, plum, cherry, and apricot—are carefully calibrated so as not to overwhelm the delicate wildflowers.

After thirty-three years in her garden, Josette de la Harpe has established a classic Santa Fe garden while adding her own personal touch—and her own layer of history—to the garden continuum.

A wildflower meadow at the summer-house gate spills over with red Icelandic poppies, yarrow, bachelor button, and coneflowers. Dwarf fruit trees, including peach and nectarine, are scaled to harmonize with the flowers. Volker de la Harpe handcrafted the massive double doors.

Classic with a twist: through the double doors seen on page 60 and opposite, de la Harpe's dramatic trademark, potted agapanthus, surrounds the pool and brings it into the garden.

The older winter-house garden has the look of a huge, romantic bouquet: at left, roses, lilacs, delphiniums, and feverfew.

Opposite, clockwise from top left: potted agapanthus; clematis brushing against an old iron pulley; white and deep orange Asiatic lilies.

Following page, a herald of spring, forsythia looks particularly vivid against neutral adobe walls and pale birch bark.

A Zen Experience

The Bartos Garden

The Japanese idea of a beautiful garden is radically different from ours. Zen gardens symbolize nature's eternal truths. Purity is the essence, and in fact the Japanese word *niwa*, or garden, means pure place. This concept finds expression in strictly formulated garden designs: austere, abstract, in harmony with the flux of time.

The formalized schemes can seem static to westerners, and we wonder where the flowers are. But the Japanese view the garden as a place of contemplation; they revere its calm as a prelude to personal enlightenment. In the carefully composed environment of universal principles, Zen gardeners feel, there comes a heightened awareness of nature's nuances—the gracefully dipping branch of a cherry tree, the tiny, vivid green shoots beside a rock. At home, the Zen garden is a private expression of spiritual and aesthetic beauty, where only the privileged guest is welcome. This is a purposeful privacy well suited to Santa Fe, where the long tradition of Spanish courtyard architecture defines intimate domains. In its deliberate austerity, a Zen garden respects the natural conditions of desert life.

A Zen garden must be in harmony with its surroundings, so it is actually appropriate anywhere, from the rainforest to the desert, says Stephen Morrel. A specialist in Zen garden design based in Chester, Connecticut, he created this garden at the East Side home of Armand and Celeste Bartos in the early 1990s. It is a dry garden (*karesansui*). The "water" in this garden is not really present, but only implied—a suggestion to spark the viewers' imagination.

The main living room of the Bartos house is sunken, waist-high with the garden, and the carefully composed scene is designed to be viewed from the picture window inside—like a painting on the wall. This scenic quality especially suits the Zen perspective of contemplation. A low door cut into an exterior wall opens onto a provocative glimpse into the garden from the gravel drive.

Despite the complex principles that guide Zen garden design, the Bartos garden is simplicity itself: small and intimate, mysterious yet extraordinarily peaceful. Closely held within adobe walls, its soothing aesthetic consists of gravel, rocks, and trees linked together in attenuated asymmetry. Gravel covers the ground, its sandy color blending with the earth-toned adobe walls to create a continuous enclosure. In this subdued environment, the individual objects in the garden come into high relief.

The traditional Japanese stones, hand-picked and placed by Morrell, radiate in a way that gives a sense of visual movement, bringing life to the whole composition. These stones also have symbolic roles to play in Zen gardens. A stone with twin peaks, for example, represents mountains. In a dry garden, stones are also set to mark the edges of a "pond" in the gravel, with a bamboo fountain indicating the invisible water's source. The trees—piñon,

Stones in the Bartos Zen garden express abstract ideals, such as the rhythm that flows from outstretched piñon branches. In this dry-style design, the gravel on the ground signifies water.

mugho pine, Russian olive, apricot, and cherry—survive from the previous owner, but Morrel has pruned them to unleash their hidden structures and energy.

In accordance with Zen principles, the garden is situated on the south side of the house. It is designed to be entered from the left with the visitor proceeding to the right, a course that mimics the progression of the life-giving sun. The narrow stone path into the garden confines the visitor with an intentional compression, a feeling quickly followed by the expansive release into the open space. The movement continues to the right, along a path of stones set in the gravel, culminating with an arching piñon tree and a stone that "receives" the movement and lifts it back into the garden, completing the cycle.

In contrast to the pure abstraction of the Zen garden in the Bartos courtyard, the garden on the other side of the house is American. Long terraced beds are laid out in graceful curves, thickly planted with rows of day lilies and lavender, that drop down to a smooth green expanse of lawn.

This garden, designed by Faith Okuma of the Design Workshop in Santa Fe, is a contrast but not a contradiction in relation to the Zen garden, explains Morrell. The Zen courtyard garden is a space defined by the adobe walls—and you cannot see much beyond those walls. So the garden is intimate and small-scale. The other side of the house is spacious and open to the distant landscape. The textures and forms in that garden open up to the textures and forms in the hills. Both are appropriate.

In the Bartos garden, East meets West, and harmony prevails.

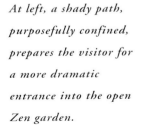

At left, a shady path, purposefully confined, prepares the visitor for a more dramatic entrance into the open Zen garden.

At right, low mugho pines bank the bamboo "fountain," which suggests a water source in the dry-style Japanese garden.

At left, sea oats in spring bring a delicate contrast to an angled stone.

Opposite, iris foliage beside a massive Russian olive tree in the snow, while a rough-hewn stone bench provides a seat for contemplation.

IN HARMONY WITH NATURE

I n contrast with the tight reins that control traditional gardens, a gentler approach seems to set the naturalistic garden free. Looser and often meadowlike, these gardens employ graceful curving beds and winding paths sympathetic to the contoured landscape. Within beds, plants are not massed in the color blocks or bands of traditional plans. Instead, colors and textures seem casually interlaced, as if the plants had magically materialized, encouraged to make themselves at home. Tall plants and short ones stand side by side, and borders blend in. Often the plants are left to seed and reseed as they will. The natural-looking garden appears to have designed itself. But the nonchalant effect is, of course, an illusion. Only a gardener possessed of ingenious artistry and superior horticultural skills can achieve such spontaneous perfection.

The rustic simplicity of naturalistic gardens is in harmony with the city and its creative inhabitants; the artful wildness of these gardens certainly captures the spirit of the place. At the same time, the more prevalent use of native plants makes these gardens "belong" to the earth. Because naturalistic gardens are grounded in nature, plants are valued for their inherent, unique characteristics. Pruning, if any, strives to reveal the plant's natural quality—not to transform it.

With a greater variety of plants and plans, natural gardens showcase a wider range of art than traditional gardens. Traditional southwestern works often appear, but in naturalistic gardens they often coexist with contemporary sculptures, and with art from faraway places.

The growing need for water-wise gardening favors naturalistic gardens that emphasize native plants. In Santa Fe, these environmentally sensitive gardens are expanding the range of beauty and possibility, affording an intense experience of nature that resonates with the challenging New Mexico landscape and climate.

The Sol y Sombra
garden (see page 104).

ACRES OF HEIRLOOMS

The Berry Garden

The rare and beautiful produce Elizabeth Berry grows at Gallina Canyon Ranch takes us back to a time when vegetables actually tasted like vegetables. A hundred years of hybridizing for transport has exacted its toll in America, but nature's own flavors still reside in the heirloom seeds that Berry collects, plants, and tends by hand. By propagating these almost-forgotten heirlooms—and treating each one as an edible work of art —she has helped bring long-lost tastes, textures, and colors back to the table.

Santa Fe's best chefs, including Mark Miller of Coyote Cafe and Katherine Kagel of Cafe Pasqual's, are finding new inspiration in Berry's stunning red tomatoes and deep yellow squash blossoms, her glossy purple Italian eggplants, Zuni watermelons, chilies and beans, kale and corn. But inspiration is a process that works both ways. Berry's love of growing is matched by the desire of the chefs to experiment, to see what new tastes they can rouse with their recipes. So she grows the specialties her chefs request of her. And in turn, they promise to try out her endless stream of experiments.

"My real love is growing rare produce so the chefs can invent new dishes and get them in front of the public," Berry says. If people don't know how delicious and healthful these specialty vegetables are, there's a great danger that many of them will become extinct. As it is, Berry estimates that five percent of our seed crop is lost every year.

Where do the seeds come from? Berry collects them wherever she can. Sometimes this means pouring over every seed catalog she finds. But equally important, people ship her seeds from all over the country; they come from old gardens, often those of the donors' grandmothers. Keeping heirloom varieties alive has become Berry's own personal quest. And this sense of mission infuses her three hundred and sixty acres with a spiritual dimension. The physical beauty of the little farm contributes to the atmosphere of otherworldliness. It spills out across a valley floor toward a view that could have been framed by Georgia O'Keeffe. Intense, flat-blue skies and jagged red sandstone cliffs paint a vivid backdrop for the lush green fields. If you imagine ancient Anasazi ruins in the mountains, you would be right.

Berry's ownership of this homestead, bordering land of the Navajo, began about ten years ago, when she bought the property and tried to raise racehorses, unsuccessfully. In the harshness of the site, she planted a flower garden, just to be able to make at least one thing bloom. And she planted a vegetable garden, just for fun. The vegetable garden started off small, so small, in fact, that only one outsider appreciated it. Fortunately, that one person was Mark Miller, the trend-setting chef from California. The year was 1985, and Miller had moved to Santa Fe to open Coyote Cafe with the aim of creating a new southwestern cuisine. He rented the house next door to Berry, and the rest is history.

The towering sandstone cliffs of Gallina Canyon are a vivid backdrop for Elizabeth Berry's bountiful garden.

Miller believes that the best-tasting, most healthful recipe depends on quality ingredients. He was quick to turn Berry's freshly picked produce into new Santa Fe specialties. Squash blossoms stuffed with fontina cheese became one of the longest running hits.

With Miller's imprimatur, Berry soon had her hands full. Requests for her produce convinced her to expand the farm, without sacrificing intimacy and personal involvement in the process. Berry does nearly everything herself, by hand. And she does it on a farm where there is no electricity, no telephone, no hot water. The gardens are watered by a gravity drip irrigation system designed by Fred Berry, an engineer. The adobe ranch house is lit by Victorian coal oil lamps and has a baby grand piano.

To make a primarily organic garden productive in the high pH soil, Berry hauls in oak leaf and pine needle mulch regularly. She plants a green manure crop each winter of annual rye and hairy vetch, to be plowed under. Compost is made from cow and horse manure. Every year, trellises are moved and a different section of the garden is planted in beans, which are plowed under before they start to make pods in order to replenish the nitrogen supply.

The climate is a challenge, for the growing season lasts only three months. Around the first of April, new seedlings are started in the greenhouse. By the first of June, they go in the ground. Greens are planted the last week in May. Toward the end of July and early August, everything explodes, ripe and ready.

The ranch has a huge perennial flower garden, adding to the overwhelming abundance that characterizes this garden. Berry's knowledge of heirloom vegetables is encyclopedic, but she professes not to know the names of any of the flowers—the hollyhocks, delphiniums, French marigolds, cosmos, and nasturtiums that provide jolts of color against the deep green expanse of the vegetable fields. However, she does name the zinnias she planted in 360-foot rows, admiring their lime-green color.

While the perennials return and the annuals blithely reseed themselves every year, Berry will be experimenting with the innovative and the traditional. She will be attendant upon the full cycle, from the seeds that she turns into wonderful plants, to their provision of inspiration for gifted chefs to create beautiful food that tastes real because it is.

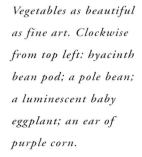

Vegetables as beautiful as fine art. Clockwise from top left: hyacinth bean pod; a pole bean; a luminescent baby eggplant; an ear of purple corn.

Opposite, Berry decorates her trusty old field truck, nicknamed "Pancho Villa," with strands of colorful chiles.

Opposite, in Berry's wild garden, the exuberant sprawl includes gloriosa daisies, a pious Madonna, and grapes of glass.

At right, above the fields, hollyhock buds are opening into blooms in the dawn light.

VISTAS AND MYSTERIES

The Balser Garden

The garden of Ron and Barbara Balser starts at the dusty street of a secluded enclave in the historic district, with an adobe wall that offers not one but two entrance gates. When the correct door swings open, a shimmery glimpse of the garden comes into view. There is an instant feeling of hushed expectation, for this first peek is filtered through the wrought iron curlicues of an old Spanish gate, then through the deep, dark shadows of a *zaguan*, a breezeway flanked by stone walls. Finally stepping out into the garden is to go from the dark to the light, and from the old world into the new.

It was that secret quality about the garden that prompted the Balsers, whose primary residence is in Georgia, to buy this house the day they saw it. "The first time I walked into the garden, I felt I was in one of those hidden gardens in Provence," Ron Balser recalls.

On the Balsers' initial visit in 1992, the house consisted of former artists' homes and studios dating back to the 1860s. Over the years, three adobe cottages had been strung together into one long, continuous dwelling. This self-contained artists' colony came with an enchanting romantic history. A particularly heartwarming story tells of Victor Higgins, an artist who visited here in 1913. He fell in love with a young girl barely in her teens; he pledged his undying love, and came back seven years later to marry her when she was of age. The sense of time and personality that came with the house still resonates. As Ron Balser says, "The character, the charm, the spirituality of this place was something we didn't find anywhere else."

The Balsers, like many Santa Fe residents, had come for a week-long vacation in 1992, and they instantly fell in love with the city, the culture, the food, and the language. They returned a few months later, bought this property, and set about making the house and garden their own.

What had been a long driveway beside the cottages is now the garden, completely enclosed within new, higher walls. The feeling of privacy is stronger than before. "From the outside, you can't see in, and from the inside, we can't see out," says Balser.

The old charm that won the Balsers' hearts lingers on. But at the same time, the garden of today is just that—a thoroughly modern space that is clean and contemporary. Tall aspen trees define a precise structure. The foliage and blooming plants have been chosen to create variety through their distinct heights, textures, and colors. And intriguing sculptures, placed to surprise, await discovery.

Santa Fe landscape architect Charles Pearson designed the garden, and he has made it seem much larger than it is. "Because the garden is small," he says, "it is all the more important that the garden have the perception of depth, and a number of vistas." The garden paths are laid out to accomplish both these goals and to serve their conventional purpose of passage as well. All visitors enter the garden on the main brick pathway, leading to the front door

A bell tower recalling Spanish mission design tops the double-gated entrance zaguan, *or passageway. Up the stairs, an Allan Houser bronze called "Love."*

beneath the portal. Then, as the path continues beyond, brick gives way to gravel, so that the tactile crunch of stones beneath the feet becomes one of the garden's private pleasures.

The path is also a sculpture walk, and the changing styles of the artworks make for distinctive feelings in different parts of the garden. The stunning stainless steel obelisk, by Georgian artist Robert Clements, is arresting in its strong silhouette; on closer inspection, it is inscribed with a poem written by the artist. "We wanted to have a little piece of Georgia here with us," Ron Balser remarks. He also notes that the sculptor was not influenced by Indian art or petroglyphs; the resemblance is coincidental even though, in this regard, the piece seems right at home in Santa Fe.

Walk to the end of the gravel path and a bronze work appears by the renowned Santa Fe artist Allan Houser. Appropriately titled "Gift of the Earth," the piece sits on stone slabs, surrounded by dense green foliage. Rounding the bend at the back of the garden, the path continues to the most eye-catching contemporary work, a tall white anthropomorphic figure by the New Orleans sculptor Ida Kohlmeyer.

The sculptures are tucked into the most intimate areas of the garden, and there are special places to stop and view each one of them. Interspersed with these major works, there are many smaller ones that add to the air of discovery: a beautifully carved bench from Mexico; a polychrome jug bearing women's faces; another Allan Houser figure at the top of the stairs; a front door painted with magnolias and wisteria; and several mezuzahs, the Jewish plaques mounted by the front gate and front door to act as a reminder of God's omnipresence and to represent the Jewish laws.

Changes of season are intriguing to see in this garden. In early spring the bulbs pop up, with their vivid color and their traditional reminder that hope springs eternal. By late May, the perennials—peonies and irises—have made an appearance, and by June the roses predominate and last through the summer. In fall the aspens turn, and in the winter the foliage is serenely beautiful in the snow.

Within this main secret garden there are more secluded gardens to discover. Next to the front gate, a tiny, walled courtyard sits off to one side. It is paved with stones, and lemon thyme covers the ground, releasing a luscious fragrance when stepped on. This garden is also planted with vines now grown to a tangle attached to the house, providing a rich, textured feeling. Another small garden at the rear of the house, off the master bedroom, is entirely private.

At left, a pear tree blooms in the spring.

Top right, the garden is planted to achieve a variety of heights, textures, and colors: aspens and fruit trees are interspersed with beds overflowing with Bishop's weed and blue Russian sage. Bottom, garden niches showcase outdoor sculptures, including Allan Houser's bronze "Gift of the Earth" in the foreground, and New Orleans artist Ida Kohlmeyer's "The Rose" on the right.

PAINTING IN FOUR DIMENSIONS

The Cohen Garden

On a mountain top north of Santa Fe, Jim and Linda Cohen have created a garden of many layers out in the "badlands." Since the couple can see Colorado from their hilltop on a clear day, the garden had nowhere to go but down the dramatic hill that slopes away from the house. Fortunately, the hillside was the perfect canvas for a labyrinthine garden design, with niches, terraces, and trails that veer off in different directions. There are so many vantage points, the viewer is looking up at the garden one minute, and down on it the next. The overall effect resembles a drawing by M.C. Escher.

The intriguing sensations created by the multiple levels are heightened by the planting—a luxurious weaving of colors and textures that covers virtually every vertical inch of the garden. Pink roses and clematis entwine themselves with each other and through the branches of the piñon trees; the columns of the portal are barely visible for the wisteria and climbing roses wrapped around them.

"This garden was nothing, just an old piñon at the bottom of the hill. We started it from scratch," says Jim Cohen, who moved to Santa Fe from New York in the early 1980s. "It's a small garden, and we've tried to make the most of it by creating terraces and by planting in layers." A former painter who now prefers to work in ceramics, Cohen regards himself as "basically a colorist" with a preference for the bolder hues. He approaches his layered garden as if he were painting in four dimensions—with the fourth dimension being time. "Of course," the experienced gardener laughs, "you have to hope the blue is still on your canvas when it's time to put on the yellow."

The Cohens have orchestrated a wonderful progression from the hilltop vista down into the cloistered seclusion of the garden. It begins at the front gate—two old wooden Mexican doors set into unadorned adobe—a few yards from the dusty, twisting road. The entrance seems plain on purpose: to ensure that when visitors enter the garden at the crest of the hill the awesome view comes as a stronger surprise. At first, then, the vista is the thing—so big and grand it takes your breath away.

"Everybody likes the mountain view," Cohen observes, "but this garden is a sheltered, secretive place. It has a way of unfolding." The garden begins to reveal itself just inside the front gates, where a gravel plateau sits next to the house on the crest of the hill. Actually more of an outdoor room, the upper level plateau is framed by the house on one side and a portal on the other. According to Cohen, this part of the garden is a result of "selective weeding," whereby he left the chamisa (now pruned like a bonsai), flax, and mullen, and

A colorist's garden includes lilies, monarda, and daisies; views of the Sangre de Cristo Mountains in the distance.

added some new plants, including blue flax, lamb's ear, hardy iceplant, and sweet peas.

From the hilltop perch, paths lead either straight ahead toward the mountain or down into the heart of the garden. The first route, toward the horizon, is a short cut to the guest house/greenhouse, a two-story structure with both a balcony and a portal that overlook the garden. A Japanese-inspired niche along this path brings the scent of water, so welcome in the desert, and the sight of a pond filled with beautiful water lilies and goldfish.

The second route catapults the visitor down a flight of steep, sweeping steps into a romantic garden enclave, a maze on three levels. The walk from the steps to the rear portal leads through layers of roses, clematis, and wisteria, past wildflowers, a vegetable garden, and stalks of cattails, culminating at the guest-house portal. It is a haven that could almost be called an English garden, but it is more accurately described as a garden modeled on English ideals.

"Our idea was to use the natural effects of our region in the way the English use box-wood, for example," says Cohen. "We were not trying to create an English garden, although the Graham Thomas roses do very well here." As part of this naturalistic approach, the Cohens designed gracefully curving beds and built the walls around the slopes. Hedges of purple euonymous cover the upper wall, topped by a bed filled with yucca. It is trimmed like an English garden. The hedges, the curved beds, the walls, and the trees establish the basic shapes, which are filled in with flowers. There are no hard edges in this garden. Wisteria wraps the portal's vertical beams and balcony rails, for example, and clematis winds its way all over the place.

The garden progresses through the seasons with one colorful flourish after another. The daffodils come in March, and parrot tulips arrive in April, when snow can still cover the ground. May is bearded iris month, which results in great masses of color punctuated by sweet rocket, also in bloom. The poppies start in late May, and by early June there are roses, hollyhocks, and delphiniums. In July, the day lilies pop open; in August there is phlox; and in September, the roses come back to bloom again.

With his garden in Santa Fe now well established, Cohen is experimenting to refine it. He is pitting aggressive plants against each other to see which one survives best. Yarrow goes head to head with monarda, and veronica spicata takes on bearded iris. No matter which wins, the result will be interesting.

Opposite, frilly hollyhocks are a counterpoint to spiky yucca and ivy-covered terrace walls.

Below, left, stairs terrace down to the protected lower garden; right, day lilies and monarda border a stepping stone path.

At left, Chicago Peace roses underplanted with blue veronica occupy the garden's lowest level, in front of the guest-house portal.

At right, bony bleached elk antlers hang like abstract sculpture above a wisteria-covered upper banister of the guest-house portal.

Opposite, a Japanese-style pond is embellished with lamb's ear and iris.

Right, clockwise from top left: Dortmond roses and lamb's ear; blue flax and iceplant line a path in the xeriscape garden; wisteria, iceplant, and blue flax next to the main house; Jupiter's beard, hollyhock, yucca, and corkscrew willow in the lower garden.

A SUBTLE MYSTERY

The Thaw Garden

A sense of mystery is always an intriguing component in the garden. Even when we know the answers, the questions still matter. Where does a path lead? Where does it end? And what is that object just barely visible around the bend?

At the home of Clare and Eugene Thaw, the classic element of mystery exists in a garden that is relatively new, not overly large, and very sophisticated. The garden was designed by Julia Berman of Eden and Wardwell in 1994 to complement a new library the Thaws had added to their house. Starting at the library's portal, a lichen-covered stone path meanders through the garden. The path traces the contour of a steep slope that is anchored by piñons and junipers, with lovely masses of plants on both sides of its meandering course. These massed plantings—tall ornamental grasses, big bursts of lavender, clouds of pink Mexican primrose—seem to draw the viewer along with their interesting combination of soft colors and strong shapes. At the rear of the garden, the path arrives at a thought-provoking focal point: an old Mexican sink nestled up to the coyote fence in a bed of daisies. The carved stone relic really looks more like a mantelpiece, a "hearth" that gives a literal twist to the idea of the garden as an outdoor living space.

As the path winds through the garden it creates a number of small niches to one side. These cul-de-sacs have an adobe wall behind them, with piñon trees and flowers in the beds. The partly shielded spaces, with their sympathetic adobe backgrounds, make ideal spots for placing artwork if the owners are so inclined—and they are. This is a collector's garden, and it was art that brought the Thaws to Santa Fe in the first place. In 1987, Eugene Thaw, a noted art dealer and collector then living in New York, was called to Santa Fe to appraise Georgia O'Keeffe's estate after her death.

The Thaws' artistic passions add another layer of mystery and interest to the design. Artworks from vastly different cultures and periods seem equally at home in this garden—and with each other. Old saddles sit atop the front gateposts as if they were on pedestals. A Moroccan jug near the gate is about to become entwined with trumpet vines inching toward it. On an adobe wall in the garden, a contemporary bronze mask with a slightly startled look appears above an Irish Gothic bench. A late-eighteenth-century baptismal font from England is used as a planter, while a bronze open sphere by Bruno Romeda, an artist who lives in the south of France, is a new piece that frames a circular view.

The garden design is special because it manages to achieve a refined combination of mystery and interest, but with a light, natural touch. "We didn't want a stiff or formal garden," says Clare Thaw. "This garden is designed for restful contemplation. All the colors are soft and natural—pinks, blues, a little lavender, and white. You'll find no red or yellow flowers here."

It is also a garden that seems spacious and cozy at the same time. "There are so many

In this collector's garden, honeysuckle spills over a Mexican stone sink, an intriguing focal point of the long view from the library portal.

interesting things going on, the garden looks much larger than it is," Berman observes. "And yet it also feels like a kindly environment—tucked in and protected," she adds. The garden is surrounded on three sides by walls and on the fourth side by the sloping hill.

The garden's sheltered location at the base of the hill, however, proved a mixed blessing in the beginning. Originally a piñon glen, the steep slope descends right down to the portal. This major change of elevation, and poor drainage in general, meant that rainwater would be effectively funneled right to the library door. Neither the Thaws nor their designer wanted to solve the site problem in the typical Santa Fe way, with terracing.

Julia Berman then set about taming the hill through her design. The piñon grove was thinned to open up the view and to give a sense of structure. Hewing to the shape of the slope, she laid a textured carpet of groundcovers—junipers, evergreens, and "evergrays"— beneath the piñons to help capture valuable water when it rains. As a perfect finishing touch to the slope, Berman added a path that spills pleasantly down to the portal. The wide, shallow steps are made of raw wood and fine gravel, and they are edged with large river stones banked with catmint for color.

The garden has a rustic sophistication that harmonizes with the new library, the last architectural work of Santa Fe's inimitable Betty Stewart. The architect, a Santa Fe legend who died shortly after the library's completion, was known to build adobe houses with a sculptural perfection—and not a straight line in the place. "Betty built things her way," Eugene Thaw recalls fondly. "I don't know how she did it, but she was always right."

The "rightness" of the library and its garden has made this area the new center of the house. And while the library is finished, the garden will be evolving for quite some time.

Opposite, a path winds the length of the garden. It outlines a slope constructed to capture valuable moisture for the plants, which include blue oat grass, catmint, hardy geraniums, junipers, and pussy toes.

At right, catmint borders steps that ease a sharp elevation, swooping gracefully down to the library portal.

Opposite, outstretched piñon branches frame a bronze mask by French artist Robert Courtright; a metal pot and Irish Gothic bench sit amid pink Mexican primrose.

The path, top right, carves out special "discovery" niches for art and flowers. Bottom right, soft colors predominate in plants such as oxeye daisies, lamium, snow-in-summer, and hardy geranium.

VISIONARIES IN THE GARDEN

Sol y Sombra

I f Sol y Sombra were simply beautiful, that would be a considerable accomplishment. These twenty acres offer up one picture-perfect vignette after another: charming fragrance gardens, rock gardens with natural grasses, an aspen grove, ponds thick with cattails, a full-to-bursting greenhouse, a vegetable garden, and endless orchards. Even the compost heap, penned in by lofty stacks of haybales, looks soft and lovely.

But beauty isn't the main point. Sol y Sombra's makers strive with a deeper purpose. They have set out to show the world (and themselves) that it is possible to transform ravaged New Mexican desert into a thriving habitat for plants and wildlife.

"This place has become a farm for growing flowers, food, people, and ideas," says Beth Miller, who with her husband, Charles Miller, owns the estate. The animating idea behind Sol y Sombra's bounty is "permaculture," a way of working with nature, rather than against it. Permaculturists seek to rediscover and restore the natural diversity and balance stamped out by the modern urge to make nature dance while man calls the tune.

But nature has usually been right all along, according to Ben Haggard, the permaculture standard-bearer who designed Sol y Sombra's gardens. Like a loving mother hen, Mother Nature has her broods—clusters of plants, animals, and insects that exist in concert, meeting each other's needs: providing food, cleaning up wastes, and assuring mutual survival. For example, corn, beans, and squash grow better together than independently. Garlic chives attract beneficial pests that keep the aphids down. Cattails filter waste water. Water draws wildlife. Harmony arises when the natural systems are restored to balance.

"Five hundred years ago, this land was covered in forests," Haggard observes. "Overgrazing by sheep turned it to scrub land subject to terrible erosion. The solution is to add what is lacking, rather than to take anything away. So when I see a 'weed,' I know it is there for a reason and I ask myself if I can find a use for it."

Sol y Sombra's success began in 1987, when Houstonians Beth and Charles Miller bought the property as their second home. The estate, whose lyrical name means "Sun and Shadow," came with a rich legacy. The rambling, Spanish-pueblo-style adobe house dates to the 1930s, and it stands out as a rare three-story adobe in a one- and two-story town. In the 1980s, Georgia O'Keeffe lived there during the last two years of her life.

Sol y Sombra's landscape, unfortunately, was not so luminous. An acre of grass spread out from the house, a water-guzzling sin in Santa Fe. Despite the extravagant lawn, the uncultivated landscape was reverting to desert, with a deepening arroyo that carried away

The vegetable garden's juniper pole gate, banked with annual sunflowers, contrasts with the contemporary greenhouse in back. This scene illustrates Sol y Sombra's intriguing duality: the modern embrace of natural ideals that yields a new horticultural vision.

valuable soil and nutrients every time it rained. "Parts of the property looked like a moon-scape," Haggard recalls.

Beth Miller was sensitive to the desert's ecology but new to its mysteries, and she liked the common-sense elegance of Haggard's permaculture ideas. Even so, testing plant propagation theories in the high desert would be a real challenge. Water is scarce, and there is no soil to speak of. These elemental necessities (which most gardeners simply take for granted) prompted Haggard to formulate two basic commandments for Sol y Sombra: "Let there be soil," and "No water shall leave this property."

The first step was small and tentative, some plantings back by the greenhouse where no one could see them. True to Haggard's prediction, the plants thrived. The permaculture experiment was on! Out came huge swaths of lawn, in went a fragrance garden planted with herbs, medicinal plants, vegetables, and antique roses—all carefully selected to be complementary. A grove of aspen trees was placed near the house. Water catchments were created by layering branches and stones over gullies. One hundred and fifty thousand shrubs and trees were planted on the property. Soil was created by laying refrigerator boxes over the ground and mulching them. A wetlands area was built to capture rainwater, and the "gray" water from the house, which is cleansed and used again to irrigate the gardens.

Now the property hums with life across all twenty acres. The rock garden teems with alpines, succulents, native perennials, and shade-tolerant species. An apothecary garden hosts edible herbs and plants like rosemary, lavender, chilies, and carrots. A classic vegetable garden feeds Sol y Sombra's residents, staff, and visitors with every edible plant Haggard was able to discover that is hardy enough to survive the climate.

The orchard—which doesn't really look like an orchard—harbors mixed plantings of fruit trees, surrounded with nitrogen-fixing herbs, shrubs, and trees. Beneficial herbs like chives, comfrey, bee balm, and tarragon go in and around the trees. Currants and raspberries grow in their shade. Edible flowers, such as day lilies, violets, and nasturtiums create a midsummer abundance. Even the insects—bees, ladybugs, wasps—and snakes and lizards are part of the plan. The greenhouse is full, bursting with tropical flowers and seedlings of edible plants.

In the wetlands, three species—cattails, reeds, and rushes—purify the water. Mixed in with them are daffodils, elderberry, primrose, marsh marigold, water iris, and horsetail. At the perimeter, native species such as piñon are coming back.

In just three years, from 1990 through 1992, Sol y Sombra has been miraculously transformed into a self-sufficient ecological wonderland, a model for solving environmental problems around the world, and a center of permaculture information. The landscape actually feels alive with the forces that are moving through it: water, wind, sun, plant life, animal life, insect life, and human beings. It looks as gorgeous as any garden, but beneath the surface the naturally balanced order takes it into another dimension. Having succeeded in making a super-abundant garden in this high desert terrain, Sol y Sombra's makers say with confidence that if permaculture can work in Santa Fe, it can work anywhere.

A rustic bench beneath a juniper-pole ramada, laden with clematis and climbing roses.

Opposite, clockwise from top left, vignettes of arts and flowers include: an Allan Houser bronze sculpture, "Taza," surrounded by columbine and hardy geranium; scarlet runner beans; another Allan Houser bronze sculpture, "Dineh," in a swath of buffalo grass; and a froth of blooms on the vegetable garden fence.

At right, near the main house, redwoods silhouette an Allan Houser bronze, "Lament."

At left, the old parking lot is now a haven for cosmos, Bells of Ireland, and sunflowers.

Opposite, a fragrant patio garden replaces a former lawn with hip-making roses, germander, and thyme-bordered stones. The bell is rung daily at lunchtime.

Following pages, amaranth, an ancient grain newly revived, fills a field in the shadow of Monte del Sol.

Opposite, pyracantha on a scrub oak trellis shows the beauty of rustic elements against adobe walls.

At right, top, the greenhouse nurtures seedlings and tender plants, including tropical angel's trumpet (hanging), and a bodhi tree whose seed was a gift of the Dalai Lama. Bottom, cosmos billows toward a rustic bench.

THE ECLECTIC SPIRIT

The passion to create, for many people, finds its best expression in the garden. And nowhere is this more true than in Santa Fe, a colony of artistic individuals distinct in this country. Within the privacy of their clay walls, Santa Fe's spirited gardeners go about making magical worlds of their own devising. Sometimes intense, sometimes playful, these gardens are testimony to the individual quests of their owners. This is the garden as dream world—a world not meant to be practical. In fact, the novelty of the idiosyncratic garden is often the point.

There is no limit to the eclectic gardener's imagination when it comes to choosing a theme—or themes. Secret grottoes, zodiac gardens, and model railroad layouts fulfill some gardeners' visions. For others, the chance to play off vastly different times and cultures is the most interesting exploration. In Mel Fillini's garden, a mix of contemporary Mexican architecture with ancient Incan iconography and Japanese minimalism produces the intriguing allure. At Andrew Ungerleider's, Buddhist imagery contrasts with southwestern woodworking and contemporary art. The creation of personal special effects—like the long drifts of pure white cosmos planted alongside Fillini's driveway to evoke snowdrifts to heaven—is a hallmark of the eccentric style.

No matter how wild the mix, how fantastic the illusion, nature is always the starting point. The most successful eclectic gardens typically begin with a "normal" traditional or naturalistic garden and take it from there. While the maker's imagination soars, the garden remains firmly grounded in structure and in the well-honed horticultural expertise of the creator. Working from a solid foundation, the eclectic gardener pursues a unique vision, perhaps breaks a few rules, and glories in the personal dream world of the garden.

The Andrew
Ungerleider garden
(see page 142).

ENGLAND JOURNEYS TO SANTA FE

The Bobbs Garden

In a town where creativity is the norm, Elspeth Bobbs infuses her garden with a super-abundant imagination. On four acres in the heart of the Canyon Road arts district, she has set among her trees and flowers an astonishing collection of garden features. There is a Santa Fe-style treehouse with its own pole ladder; a working model railroad made realistic with dwarf junipers and sedums along its route; a secret grotto banked with day lilies; a home-made scarecrow in the vegetable patch; and a pet cemetery for the family's canines loved and lost. The little departed ones are memorialized with a plaque bearing a Latin inscription *Sit sibi terra levis*, "May the earth lie on you lightly." In her garden, Bobbs turns the proverb upside down. Her expansive garden rests lightly on the earth, respectful of the land's sensitivity, while providing a natural outlet for the whimsical side of her personality.

The playful quality that characterizes this garden belies the seriousness of its maker, who is a lifelong gardener. Today, the garden is one of the oldest and largest in the city. Seeing the robust fullness that results from thirty years of informed attention, it is surprising to learn that the gardener and the garden first engaged each other across a vast cultural and horticultural divide.

A native of England and a barrister by profession, Bobbs began a new life in Santa Fe when she moved here in 1967 with her husband, Howard, a prominent watercolor painter attracted to the city's burgeoning artist colony. The house and studio fulfilled the dream of proximity to Canyon Road and its concentration of artists and galleries. But while the property was substantial and nicely elevated, with a pretty, gentle slope toward the Santa Fe River below, the ground itself was hardscrabble and forlorn, barely supporting a few rangy old fruit trees.

Before she came to Santa Fe, Bobbs had made many gardens in England, a land of deeply entrenched gardening ideals fit for a place that is cool, wet, and formal. Her hard-won English expertise demanded serious reconsideration in the new environment, which suffers from extreme heat and cold, unquenchable dryness, and has scant gardening tradition to fall back on. Using trial and error as her guides, Bobbs embarked on the adventure of inventing a new gardening tradition all her own.

Even so, there is a little more of England here than you might think possible. The English acceptance of the idea of the garden room, for example, proved to be a helpful organizing principle for this four-acre garden—especially since adobe walls surround the property. Inside these walls, Bobbs has created a series of individual gardens, each with a

A cross atop a weathered gate encircled by winter jasmine in Elspeth Bobbs's garden.

distinct and usually lighthearted theme: a medieval garden, a railroad garden, and a zodiac garden planted in a dozen sections. Long, heavily planted beds—many with lovely perennial borders of salvias, anthems, lilies, larkspur, poppies, and asters—line the paths and mark transitions between the garden areas.

Reminders of England also arise in the knot garden, a traditional version of the British classic that is among the best in the city. Another beloved English tradition, the herb garden, also appears, with a wealth of herbs selected for their intriguing fragrances—lemon verbena, pineapple sage, rosemary, thyme, tarragon, and many more—and these scented herbs often permeate her cooking. There is also a formal English-style garden, where roses grow in profusion, among them hybrid teas and old and new David Austins. The most recent addition to the garden, a lovely *ramada*, is planted with climbing roses, clematis, and wisteria that add height and soft color near the house.

Set off at a distance from the flower gardens lies Bobbs's vegetable garden. This sizable plot is filled with corn, broccoli, beans, spinach, and red cabbages. An early convert to organic growing, Bobbs has been composting here since the 1970s, a factor she credits for her successful produce.

A life of art appreciation also inspires these glorious gardens. Almost every garden area displays a local artist's work. While the artworks never overwhelm the plantings, these statues and sundials, and numerous murals by David Roe, make it clear that this is a Santa Fe garden.

While it was never Bobbs's intention to faithfully re-create the garden styles of her native England, she has found over the years that in her own way she has made a garden that unites the best of both worlds.

Opposite, impish figures in the rose garden show this serious gardener's playful side; the low groundcovers include thyme and dwarf conifers.

At right, day lilies and trumpet lilies in the perennial garden.

Opposite, artemesia, sage, and other fragrant herbs scent this southwestern-style courtyard, which is decorated with wagon wheels, bleached skulls, Victorian-style settees, and St. Francis in a planting of mint.

At right, succulents spill over the headpiece of a Mexican terra-cotta figure.

THE ECLECTIC SPIRIT

Scenes from Bobbs's four-acre garden, opposite, clockwise from top left: a Madonna oversees impatiens, glass balls, and a grinding stone; impatiens bloom in a terra-cotta character's brow; dried yarrow brushes against a trompe l'oeil painted cabinet; morning glories invade a sundial.

At right, in the far garden an old mill stone is banked by candy tuft in front and Louisiana sage behind; the fruit tree arches toward a Madonna above a basin.

At left, the rough-hewn treehouse pole ladder.

A new rose garden, opposite, top, blooms with colorful David Austin roses; climbing varieties cover the ramadas. *Bottom, Elspeth Bobbs's Victorian-style perennial garden showcases delphiniums, day lilies, and a wrought-iron settee.*

AT THE TOP OF THE HILL

The Cash Garden

It is often said that in terms of gardening and architecture, Santa Fe is a lot like Afghanistan. The two places share similar desert climates and extremely high altitudes, and the buildings and plants of Afghanistan work equally well in Santa Fe. Perhaps that is why the intricately carved gate at Dianne and Berry Cash's home seems so perfect here. While it indeed comes from Afghanistan, the tradition of carved wooden gates is common to both locales. Painted a searing cobalt blue, this gate is strong enough to dominate a sandy hilltop and to hold its own against the vast blue of the sky.

The sight of the gate is so striking that a visitor confronting it for the first time might fail to notice the rest of the scene: how favorably the house is situated on top of a mountain, appearing to have the whole world to itself. Even after the gate swings open, the fortuitous siting is withheld for a moment. First, there is an expansive courtyard where graceful piñons shade beds of dusty pink Jupiter's beard, red oriental poppies, coral bells, delphiniums, and other intensely colorful perennials. Small patches of lawn contribute to the feel of the courtyard as a cool oasis sparked by hot colors. Looking through this interesting array of flowers and trees, the visitor can begin to take in the length and breadth of the view.

Stone paths lead from the gate to the central patio at the top, which has big comfortable chairs and an outdoor fireplace. This courtyard, with the house on one side and the guest house on the other, is clearly designed for entertaining and for informal family gatherings.

The Cashes are Dallas natives who have traveled widely, putting together extensive collections of furniture and objects from their travels over the years. Large Moroccan jugs lean against the blue front gate; in the courtyard, Mexican pottery decorates the fireplace.

At the swimming pool on the opposite side of the house, there is another comfortable patio with a massive outdoor fireplace and a display of pottery and artifacts. This is the wild, uncultivated side of the house, where the "garden" of petunias and marigolds grows in containers. On this side, the land has been turned over to a vast wildflower meadow that stretches out to the distant horizon with clover, prairie cone flowers, cosmos, and yarrow in a field of blue gramma grass.

Every part of the garden reveals a slice of the view. It is only by climbing a ladder to the roof of the two-story guest house that it is possible to see it all at once, three hundred and sixty degrees of big sky country.

The central courtyard is the Cashes' favorite "room" in the house, with the garden on one side and the breathtaking landscape view on the other.

Opposite, delphinium, snow-in-summer, and potentilla border a stone path leading around the side of the house.

At right, top, searing blue paint is flaked to perfection on the main entrance gate, flanked by hollyhocks and jugs from Morocco. Bottom, roses and delphiniums fill the front flower beds along the entrance drive.

Cash garden close-ups, clockwise from top left: delphinium by a window; petunias and marigolds in pots by the pool; lychnis and other perennials in beds, and potted geraniums in the main courtyard; potted petunias near another boldly painted gate.

Opposite, dwarf burning bush viburnum makes a blazing background for two Santa Fe icons: a terra-cotta vase with lizards on it and a bleached skull.

At left, a little red climbing rose is a natural complement to those forged into the embellished iron cross.

Opposite, curvaceous Moroccan jugs and hollyhocks soften the brilliant blue entrance gate.

ANOTHER WORLD

The Fillini Garden

The magic in Mel Fillini's garden is created through a fascinating fusion of cultures. The face of an Incan sun god dominates the garden gate; the smooth stones on the bridge look Japanese; and the water cascading from the high canal is a homage to Mexican architect Luis Barragan. Ancient longings, distant ideals, and modern visions: somehow they all coherently commingle. The garden combines these times and worlds to become, in turn, a world of its own.

Far from the garden proper, a meadow of hot pink cosmos marks the start of a long gravel drive that climbs gently to the house. This entry point is on higher ground, so the first glimpse of property comes though the flowers. The colored cosmos give way to the white ones that line both sides of the driveway, framing postcard views of the mountains in the distance. "We wanted people to approach the house as if they were driving through snow drifts," explains Fillini. Like most scenic routes, this one takes visitors the long way around—past the house, to the garden gate some distance beyond, then through the garden, and back toward the house.

Both the garden and the adobe house were designed by Ron Robles, who worked in Mexico with Barragan in the 1960s. In recounting the process of creating this garden, Robles remembers that the owner's personality was the key. "Mel Fillini likes to garden and he likes to entertain. We wanted to evoke a fantasy world. When we started in 1981, there were only a few scruffy trees and a small stone granary building from the 1830s," Robles explains. "We wanted the house to go with the garden. But we did the garden first, and then we designed the house around it."

"Doing the garden" turned out to be a three-year endeavor that proceeded by increments, and by intuition, on the two-and-a-half acre property. "The gates, the walls—they grew as the garden grew," Robles recalls. "The drama, the intimacy, and the scale of the garden have been woven throughout as we went along." One feels this integration amid the graceful curving beds and paths that wind through the garden's center. The beds are packed with flowers, so there are many tempting opportunities to pause and smell, touch, or simply look. Even though the garden is large, it is divided into three terrace levels, where small groups of people can comfortably gather.

Scale is established by the trees—hundreds of aspen, piñon, fruit, and other species. "Planting these trees was an extremely important goal in this garden," Robles says. The property is located in a barren valley once filled with trees. "All the nursery people said to forget it, that the trees would never grow here again." Now the wind rustles softly through the canopy of leaves, and people driving along the far mountain ridge stop to admire the aspen turning gold in the fall.

At this elegantly architectural residence, the garden design actually came first, and the house was built around it. Tulips and aspen border a flagstone path linking the two.

At left, top, the entrance drive is lined with white cosmos to simulate snow. Bottom, lilacs screen the main garden terrace, with its Barragan-style fountain and pool, spanned by a deck with Japanese influences.

Opposite, a metal sculpture by Ron Robles rises above terraced beds filled with columbines and day lilies; aspens are among hundreds planted for shade.

THE ECLECTIC SPIRIT

Opposite, the Barragan-inspired fountain makes art of its function, capturing and recirculating rainwater. The locust tree is embellished with Ron Robles's wind chimes.

At right, an Inca sun god's face adorns the main entrance gate in a free-standing wall. This provocative entrance is located beyond the garden, creating a pleasant promenade through the garden to the front door.

THE SOUND OF WATER

The Ungerleider Garden

In Santa Fe's high desert climate, the presence of water has an almost mystical appeal to parched senses. It is always an alluring thing to see, and to hear. At the entrance to Andrew Ungerleider's garden, a small pond and a narrow stream lie just inside a juniper fence. The soft trickling tones of the water drift easily beyond the fence and over the street. Visitors can hear the soothing sound before the source is seen, and the music of the water provides a heightened feeling of anticipation.

Once the double fence-doors swing open, the garden makes good on its promise with no further ado. A stream edged with river rocks flows just inside the garden gates. The water burbles underfoot as visitors cross a little footbridge set into a lichen-covered cut-stone path. The stream feels cool and shady, and it seems a million miles away from the hot, dusty street on the other side of the fence.

The oval-shaped pond provides the wellspring that feeds the stream. It is to the right of the path, near the portal, and nestled beneath a shade tree. Water lilies float lazily on the surface. Tall, arching plants—including day lilies, irises, and ornamental grasses—help to slow evaporation and lend an oasis air to the whole front garden.

"One of my favorite aspects of this garden is its contrast with the outside," says Julia Berman of Santa Fe's Eden and Wardwell, who designed it. "You open the gate, go through a coyote fence, and there you are—in an enchanting garden. The water is right there."

Beyond the stream, it is clear that the Ungerleider yard has been transformed into the Ungerleider garden. What lawn remains is small enough be ecological, but large enough to provide a deep green counterpoint to the floral color. And what a glorious color palette it is: velvety magenta, inky purple, pale violet, soft golden rose, warm yellow, and a little hot orange for spice—with some white here and there for visual cooling. In summer there is a procession of plants spilling over the winding path: catmint, day lilies, dianthus, California poppies, pyrethrum, columbines, salvia, thyme, centranthus, and Johnson's blue geranium.

Ungerleider loves lots of flowers, and it shows in the front garden especially. "He wanted flowers all the time—a succession of color, a succession of bloom, these were his wishes," Berman recalls. "If we could have had one of each flower in the universe, I think he would have been overjoyed."

Many of the garden's trees and shrubs blossom in their season. Lilacs and crab apples, for example, add a canopy of blossom; along with the irises and the floribunda roses, they contribute to the lushness that is classic East Side Santa Fe.

The garden's design also offers a change of scene. The carefully balanced composition of the front yard changes to a wild meadow at the side of the house. These two gardens are different in spirit, and they reside on split levels. The front yard occupies the high ground, with

Small amounts of water bring a cool, shady feel to the more traditional front garden. The plants—an apple tree, blue oat grass, day lilies, juniper, and irises— lend a classic East Side Santa Fe look.

the wilder garden on the lower level, and a stone retaining wall dividing them. A small waterfall is created by the change of elevation, adding more soothing sounds of water. Berman has planted a dense grove of aspen, amur maples, and other trees near the transition point to give a sense that change is at hand.

Beyond the wild meadow, the garden turns formal again. Within an adobe-walled garden area stretch perennial beds filled with day lilies, prairie cone flowers, annual sunflowers, and primroses. Colors are still on the bright side, but with a subtle shift. Berman describes her palette for the back garden as "primary colors, one step off: brilliant blues, magenta, and hot orchids, together with pinks, golden yellows, plus white."

The split-level design of Ungerleider's garden succeeds in several ways. It permits stylistically different gardens to coexist in harmony. It takes advantage of a hillside location to channel the movement of a flowing stream throughout the garden. And perhaps best of all, it performs a welcome magic trick: opening the view to the distant mountains, and at the same time creating a secluded sanctuary oblivious to the busy street just outside its garden gates.

Opposite, in fall, aspen leaves turn brilliant gold.

At right, in mid-summer, blue oat grass and columbine contribute seasonal color.

Opposite, clockwise from top left: in the front garden, a long-faced stone sculpture from Easter Island; Jupiter's beard, hardy geraniums, iris, cat-mint, and an apple tree near the pond; purple cone flowers and catmint near a bust of Buddha from Indonesia; and day lilies near the guest-house portal.

At right, wisteria climbs the pergola that leads to the back yard's wild meadow; thyme fills the spaces between pavers.

Top, day lilies and cone flowers bank the pond. Bottom, the Asiatic lily, Luxor, tangles together with catmint and ivy in the front beds.

Opposite, near the lower pond, creeping thyme (both red and lemon) and lamium "Beacon Silver" cover the ground.

The Art of the
Garden

A rt, and art appreciation, comprise the coin of the realm in Santa Fe. An artist's colony of international renown, the city has a long-standing reputation for loving art. Today, almost everyone in town is involved: painters, sculptors, printmakers, photographers, writers, artisans and crafts people, gallery workers, and collectors. Here, the integration of art and life is virtually total. This vibrant ambiance naturally flavors the gardens, where a love of beauty provides the basic impulse behind every creation.

Fine art, folk art, sculpture, religious art, murals, and crafts—Santa Fe gardens have it all. The more formal gardens tend to have formal art such as large sculptures around the grounds, like an open-air gallery. In formal gardens, figurative works are especially prized. Local sculptors such as Glenna Goodacre, Allan Houser, and Dan Ostermiller are creating works that introduce contemporary versions of traditional southwestern themes into Santa Fe's gardens.

But quirkier folk styles generally prevail. This artwork cheerfully celebrates the glory of simple materials and methods: stamped tin, pressed glass, clay, ceramics, even straw. Hand-carved wooden statues and religious icons reside among flowers and trees. Colorful murals depict southwestern scenes or bold geometric designs reminiscent of Native American blankets. Statues, plaques, and little shrines are mounted right on the adobe walls; cut-out windows form views, like paintings rivaling Georgia O'Keeffe's.

For artists, the garden is a place to create art and display it. Like Monet at Giverny, many artists plant their gardens in order to paint them. But the combination of art and the garden reaches its ultimate conclusion at the Dickenson home, where the entire garden has been conceived as a work of art.

The Ford Ruthling
Garden (see page 152).

SANTA FE BAROQUE

The Ruthling Garden

In Santa Fe, most people say a hilltop house is best—those views of endless earth touching boundless sky never fail to take your breath away. But Ford Ruthling is not one of these people. To his mind, the intimacy of his own garden, which slopes down a gentle rise to a rambling Territorial-style adobe house, is infinitely better.

As it is, this secluded garden reveals itself in a series of beautiful increments. Ruthling's private world exists a few blocks from the city's historic central Plaza, but no one passing by would suspect it. The property is well hidden from the street, tucked out of sight on an interior lot. It is reached by a length of gravel drive that would also be invisible except for the long coyote fence, edged with orange day lilies, that runs alongside. The driveway leads to another coyote fence, this one entwined with lilacs, which shields the garden view. Then, even before the garden can be seen, a symphony of sound catches the ear. Classical music or opera is always billowing out over these three acres, a clarion call that there is life inside, and plenty of it.

The garden gate leads to a walkway that terraces down three levels of a magnificently profuse garden surrounding the house. But first, the gate provides a few strong hints about the garden and the personality of its maker. A bright blue door blazes in a freestanding adobe wall that is framed by a pink-blossomed nectarine tree cascading over the top; on the left, the wall is inset with a lion's head plaque cast in bronze. Yes, art is imitating life once again. The owner is an artist, an impressive man who is leonine in stature. As he roams around this garden he has been making for more than twenty-five years, he seems like a lion at home in his lair.

Ford Ruthling is well known as a painter, and over the years he has also trained himself in the old local craft of hammering tin into works of art. Ruthling's creative affluence is such that everything he touches turns to art. This garden is an alternate palette, one that allows the artist to intermingle important aspects of his life, his work, and his heritage as a native of Santa Fe. It is a palette that is constantly changing.

Hardly a day goes by that this gardener-artist is not overseeing his evolving creation, with new variations always on his mind. Some days will find him installing an artwork of his own creation, like the bronzed man in the half-moon face that sits atop a pole in the cutting garden. At other times, he will concentrate on the folk art of old and New Mexico that he has been collecting for decades. As a son of Santa Fe, Ruthling feels a deep attachment to these artisan treasures—the benches, chairs, lamps, and the rare Peñasco doors with their cut-out panels, to name a few—and they often find their way into the garden. The garden affords Ruthling the opportunity to display his art and artifacts amid masses of plantings, and this is clearly one of its most important delights.

The main entrance to Ruthling's "garden of rooms" is a bright blue wooden gate in a freestanding adobe wall, guarded by a lion's head and a pot full of geraniums.

At the heart of the garden, of course, is Ruthling's passion for plants. There is a tumultuous abundance of flowers, and they sport many colors: California poppies in pinks, reds, and oranges; irises in deep purples and pale yellows; bright yellow daffodils; purple-blue delphiniums; day lilies in yellows, oranges, and pinks; cosmos in both pink and white varieties; white and yellow yarrow; many-colored roses; tall yellow sunflowers—and this is just the start of it. These plants tumble over the walkways and tangle around the art pieces in a happy array, and, in some cases, an equally happy disarray.

According to Ruthling, the mythical principles of garden design—the need for focal points and axes—may be just that: myths. He says his garden doesn't have these standards, and yet he finds it completely satisfactory without them.

Even so, there is an underlying structure to the place that keeps the floral explosions under tentative control. The natural slope of the terrain has been segmented into three terrace levels, and the gardens are loosely arranged into a series of garden rooms on the different levels. Large old fruit trees, including nectarines, apricots, and crabapples, plus plentiful evergreens, add height and sturdiness around the perimeter, and in the garden's interior as well. Finally, the adobe buildings on the property—the rambling red-roofed main house, a garage and three guest houses—contribute a series of walls that act as visual boundaries behind all the flowers.

When he moved to this property in 1970, Ruthling started the garden in the interest of both work and play. The flowers he planted became subjects for his paintings, and the garden gave him a place to rest his eyes from the canvas. In time, the art progressed to other subjects, like the 1977 pueblo pots that appeared as U.S. postage stamps. And the garden evolved into a place of pure enjoyment.

The pleasure of this place continues beyond the daylight hours. Ruthling sometimes awakes at midnight and walks around his garden in the moonlight. And even though he no longer paints the flowers that surround him, he insists that it is his talent as a painter that made his garden possible: "I have this land, I have this garden, and it all comes from the painter in me."

Opposite, Ruthling's "floppy" poppies, roses, and bearded iris explode with color, while an adobe wall adds architectural interest.

At right, a coyote fence separates the front gate from beds of delphiums and columbines in the rambunctious inner garden.

At left, fresh cut iris
and California poppies
enliven an eccentric
tableau of haunting
folk art and a carved
wooden cabinet on the
patio.

Opposite, old glass
bottle bottoms are inset
in the patio wall; the
blue pot is by Mexican
artist Dolores Hidalgo,
and the hanging glass
grapes are from India.

In his garden, Ruthling creates flamboyant scenes, like this blue pole, at left, decorated with the artist-gardener's tin cutouts and placed in a bed of "floppy" poppies. His artistic touch is evident throughout the garden.

Opposite, clockwise from top left: lovebirds cut out of wood; a birdhouse of tin-trimmed wood; a brightly painted hand-carved wooden screen; cut-tin birds.

At left, a metal rooster leans against the "chicken house" wall.

Opposite, oriental poppies bloom outside the old chicken house, which was turned into a guest house.

AN ARTISTIC CLOISTER

The Anthony Garden

Big, airy tumbleweeds come to rest beneath the branches of beautifully pruned piñon trees on Carol Anthony's windswept land, yet her five-acre compound seems not so much southwestern as medieval. The earthen, homemade structures—including a thatched-roof *sanctuario* within a walled garden—have clearly been inspired by the idea of an ancient monastery.

At first glance the simple buildings and their gardens appear quite austere, but on closer inspection they reveal the fine, hand-decorated intricacy of an illuminated manuscript.

This is, in fact, a modern pilgrim's home and garden, a place of refuge and of new beginnings. Carol Anthony, an artist, journeyed here to live alone in an artistic refuge of her own devising. Opportunities for solitude and for contact with the land had been too long lacking in New York City, despite her successful artistic career. Anthony's paintings portray dense, moody landscapes outside of time, and she sought a solitary, timeless environment that would be in sympathy with her work. Here, in the open country south of Santa Fe, she found the qualities of peaceful serenity she was searching for in her spiritual quest.

"This is the way the land is supposed to be," Carol Anthony declares, "soft, wild, and free."

The dream of an artistic sanctuary began, appropriately, with a garden. For many years, Anthony envisioned a place that would be her personal cloister—a combination of an ancient monastery and an old New Mexico *sanctuario,* a vital remnant of a mythical past. In the dream it was always the same: a walled courtyard garden with a straw-bale *casita* and a thatched-roof *sanctuario* on the grounds. The desire for the cloister proved so compelling that she built this part of the compound even before the "main" house, the small home and studio on the compound's grounds where she lives and works today.

While Anthony covets her solitude, she is by no means a recluse. A group of friends joined her in constructing the straw-bale buildings with their own hands—like an old-fashioned barn-raising stretched out over three years. It was a process of mixing mud, plastering walls, and thatching the roof, a process Anthony recalls as spurred on by laughter and a few shots of tequila every now and then.

These walls seem proud to show their earthy origins, and you can see flecks of straw in the dark-brown adobe. And while the cloisters' structures may be tiny, they impart a satisfying sense of solidity and kindly spirits. The one-room *casita* has only 400 square feet and an adobe floor. A lovely front porch is embellished by an old Mexican door and shutters, and by Anthony's signature painted *retablos* inset into the outside walls.

Across the courtyard, near the cloister gate, sits the thatched-roof *sanctuario,* with a pair of nineteenth-century pitchforks flanking its miniature entry. The natural roof is a highlight of the little building, but it succumbs to the weather and has to be redone four times a year. Flower beds along the *casita*'s front porch are banked with lavender, Russian sage, and

Anthony's affinity for spherical life-forms turns to reverie in this porchside vignette. The little tabernacle sits on a pillow beneath the artist's pear painting, inset into the adobe wall.

artemesia. These plantings are still evolving, but a constant focal point is a campfire and a large table surrounded by straw bales where Anthony gathers her friends in the cool of the evening. A white tablecloth always covers the table, signifying communion with her friends, with her art, and with the earth.

"Finally having the cloister was like a homecoming for me," Anthony says, "even though I was living here for the first time. It was the fulfillment of my own dream of paradise—my art, my animals, and my personal belongings all in one place."

Because the cloister fulfills so many of Anthony's wishes, it is much more than a garden devoted to plants. The entire compound has evolved into a testament to her artistic spirit and her relationship to the land. A vital part of this relationship is the way the compound fits into the whole natural life cycle: the straw that grows in the fields has been recycled as a building material; the perennials reseed themselves; nothing is wasted; and life goes on.

Solitude and memory are well served in this garden, but it is also a garden that delights the senses. Fragrance, for example, has received careful consideration. Plants are judiciously placed to capture their scents, like the sweet-smelling jasmine twining up a post beam of the front porch near her favorite rocking chair.

The garden is also a counterpoint to Anthony's traveling life. She spends her summers in England, near Sissinghurst, steeped in the damp greenness she finds to be the perfect balance to the bone-dryness of her Santa Fe home.

Carol Anthony has achieved a highly elusive ideal—her art and her life are completely integrated. Her dream world has become her real world. It is an exact replica of herself, and everything here bears a signature stamp: her colors, her poignant and timeless style, her fullness of spirit.

Opposite, the straw bale sanctuario *pays homage to the medieval monastery. (Anthony rethatches its roof several times yearly.) The nineteenth-century hay rakes are from England and France.*

At right, friends often gather around tables and chairs in the low-walled sanctuario *courtyard.*

At right, honeysuckle reaches out to the coyote-fence gate, while geraniums, Russian sage, blue mist spirea, and chamisa grow nearby.

Opposite, top, beds that line the casita's portal have an ethereal silvery blue sheen; plants include Russian sage and Louisiana sage. Bottom, Anthony's trompe l'oeil painted window scene combines with real-life campanula draped from a window box, and blue mist spirea in the bed.

Anthony's gift for making art out of everyday objects, clockwise from top left: a tin shrine on the wall above a crate of buffalo gourds; a tin farm-style pitcher with cut flowers; a vase of dried statice beside one of Anthony's framed pear insets; a bowl of buffalo gourds.

Opposite, a wooden gate between thick straw-bale walls evokes Anthony's conception of a southwestern "medieval" monastery. Terra-cotta stars suggest heaven on earth.

LOOKING IN

The Matteucci Garden

Hardly a day goes by that Nedra and Richard Matteucci don't find someone gazing into their garden. Almost every gallery goer on Canyon Road strolls right past it, and it is impossible not to be intrigued. The front gates are mysterious and a little wild-looking. They're often left open, exposing a cool green garden reverberating with hot spots of color and punctuated with enough glimmering bronze statuary that it could be another gallery that will welcome visitors in. Even tour buses sometimes stop here by mistake.

But when the gates are closed, the garden once again becomes the Matteuccis' private world—an elegant domain that reflects the restoration of a special Santa Fe home and the planting of a garden where there was once just a yard.

The garden was conceived in 1992 by the Matteuccis and their landscape architect, Robert Johns, to be a contemporary complement to one of the oldest residences in Santa Fe. With a main house dating to the 1860s, and a jacal (now a guest house) from the 1700s, the Matteuccis found themselves entrusted with an important piece of Santa Fe's past. In exploring their new-found home, they were amazed to discover a Diego Rivera tile mural— it had been hidden behind a clump of overgrown ivy on the front garden wall and long since forgotten.

With this rich heritage, Nedra Matteucci "wanted the garden to look like it had always been here." Given the property's fascinating history, she felt "it was important to do some reclamation—but not to do too much too soon. The approach to the garden had to be gradual."

The Matteuccis have created their garden as a series of spaces with plentiful color. There is a front garden near the street; an open lawn for croquet and boccie games; a patio with space for eating outdoors; a pond and stream with a natural meadow; and a separate garden at the back of the property. Figurative sculpture provides the artistic continuity. There are lifelike statues of people, including Glenna Goodacre's "Jill," and a solemn Indian woman ("Daka's Rattle") by Doug Hyde. There is also a menagerie of animal figures: a ram by Floyd DeWitt; a rooster by Jane De Decker; Dan Ostermiller's "Le Toad" and turtle in the pond, and his mysterious ravens in the trees.

The garden is large enough to have many microclimates. The Matteuccis and their gardener, Dana Rice, have seized on these pockets of opportunity to diversify the plantings in a way that keeps the garden interesting year round—even in winter. It has become a "garden of discovery," and Rice is always planting "a little this and a little that to see how the plants work together." This method, he admits, turns out to be far more involved than any garden plan, but also more interesting and fun. He often mixes vegetables, herbs, and flowers in the same bed, for example, and if a volunteer specimen shows up, so much the better. Weeds are

Behind the Matteuccis' Territorial-style house, parts of which date to the 1700s, the pond creates a naturalistic oasis lush with raven grass, papyrus, and water lilies.

tolerated too. "They're green and they're lush," Rice notes. "I just have to get them out before they go to seed."

The idea of gradual evolution for the garden has proven to be a solid concept, and the constant and vigilant attention to progress has made for a provocative garden. By working gradually, the Matteuccis and their gardener have made more than a garden. They have established an ecosystem that attracts wildlife. In the summer, an invasion of butterflies occurs, although it only lasts for a day or two. Hundreds of birds arrive in the fall.

The Santa Fe "season" starts early in this garden. In February, with everyone already tired of winter, daffodils and tulips burst out with great splashes of color. Even though snow might still blanket the ground, crocuses will crop up across the middle lawn. Later, the roses and delphiniums bloom, and the spectacular grape-scented irises. The back garden is filled with old roses that flower in summer. In the fall the aspen groves shower the garden with their yellow leaves.

This is a garden that never goes out of season. There is always something going on, even in winter. Evergreens keep their color, the trees lose their leaves, and the garden opens up to show its underlying structure. The sculpture, always a delight in this garden, takes on an ethereal prominence.

Opposite, a rare English walnut tree in Santa Fe.

At right, a serene limestone sculpture, "Daka's Rattle," by Doug Hyde, is surrounded by Lady's Bells; silver lace vine covers the fence.

THE ART OF THE GARDEN

Opposite, top, a faux wishing well with holly-hocks. Bottom, a lichen-covered stone sits in a bed of daffodils.

At right, a bronze sculpture, "Jill," by Glenna Goodacre, with coleus in the foreground.

Opposite, perennials beside the stream include ornamental onions and lupines.

At right, Matteucci's long-buried treasure, a tile mural by famed Mexican artist Diego Rivera, which was discovered beneath a decades-old blanket of ivy.

THE INSTINCTIVE GARDEN

The Havard Garden

To artist James Havard, making a garden is the same as painting a picture. It's something best left to instinct.

"I do the garden by eye," he says, "the same way I paint." He has an interesting point. Like oil paint on canvas, plants have a malleable quality. "If you plant something that doesn't work out, you can always move it."

The Havard garden is only seven years old, but already it is a wild and wonderful place. There are clouds of wildflowers and outbursts of grasses. There are multi-trunked piñons and masses of perennials. There are winding paths where flowers brush against your legs and a waterfall that spills into a pond. There are gargoyles from Europe everywhere you look. With such exuberance, the garden seems on the verge of overflowing the adobe walls, but a series of terraces and beds keeps it tethered. "I always overdo the garden a little, just in case," Havard admits.

And why not? This garden is an antidote to his former life in New York in a Tribeca loft. Havard, whose works are owned by the Metropolitan Museum of Art and the Museum of Modern Art in New York, is among those artists who moved to Santa Fe in stages. He had been traveling to the city for years in search of Native American folk art. On the walls of his Tribeca loft, the artist's abstract canvases mingled with an increasing number of folk art pieces and furniture: beadwork, quillwork, kachinas, Hopi masks, and parfleches (rawhide pouches for holding arrows).

Then, after more than a decade as a visiting collector in Santa Fe, the artist finally came to stay. "I was drawn to the light, and to the incredible blue skies," says Havard.

In Santa Fe, the Havard property covers five acres, and the part devoted to gardening caps a little knoll behind the house. It shows the results of the artist's eye—and hand—for gardening by instinct. The garden also shows how the artist's intuition blends artifacts of European, Native American, and contemporary cultures into a domain that could only exist in Santa Fe. A lovely seventeenth-century four-panel gate from France becomes an icon in its arched adobe frame. At the far end of the garden, across from the French gate, there is a complementary opening in the adobe wall, with a simple white cross above the door. A tiny, free-standing adobe "chapel" to one side is pure New Mexico. All around the garden Havard has placed gargoyles from Europe, but he has mixed them in with pottery planters from the southwest.

By instinct, or by design, the garden works from one end to the other. Doing a "little something every year," his creation not only looks right, it also feels right. Like a fine painting, it bathes the spirit. "It's incredibly relaxing to be in this garden," says Havard. "I always say I don't have to pay a psychiatrist as long as I have it. For me, it's very good therapy."

In the artist's back garden, southwestern architectural forms meet European artifacts along a path planted with blue oat grass, phlox and other perennials, and aspen trees.

Top, an urn banked in baby's breath overlooks a gate with a view toward Sun and Moon Mountains. Bottom, the garden here is higher than the house; blue oat grass and marigolds are among the plants beside the hillside path leading to the main gate.

Opposite, the main gate seems Mexican, but its provenance is actually seventeenth-century France.

The garden's intimacy
contrasts with the space
beyond the walls.
In a protected corner,
roses, baby's breath, and
Russian sage grow
beneath an aspen tree.

Opposite, mint makes a
cool background for a
sculptural fragment.

NEW WAVE

The Dickenson Garden

To walk into Nancy Dickenson's courtyard garden for the first time is a startling experience, a shock to the system of accepted garden ideas. What is this amazing place? There are traces of traditional gardens—trees, fountains, climbing trumpet vines, and colorful pots of petunias. But could this creation really be called a garden? Or have we discovered an artwork of garden proportions? Actually, it is a cross between the two: an original work of contemporary art that covers the ground instead of the walls.

"At first I thought about doing a normal garden and buying a sculpture or something and plopping it in," says Nancy Dickenson. "But I realized I'd have much more fun by turning the whole garden into the art."

A garden of bagels flashed in her mind. In Boston she had seen this concoction, a yard filled with round dough balls painted purple and green. It was designed by Martha Schwartz, the Boston-based landscape architect and artist, who was only half joking. Schwartz, the Andy Warhol of landscape architecture, is a "new wave" artist who treats the garden as a pop art event. Nancy Dickenson is an artist and collector herself. She recognized that Martha Schwartz's artistic approach would lead to the visionary garden of her dreams.

"I said to Martha, 'You are the artist. I would like for you to make my entire garden a piece of conceptual art,'" Dickenson explains. But this did not mean that the garden was to be a vision created in artistic isolation. "Martha asked me what my favorite shape was, and I said the spiral. Then she asked me what garden elements I loved. I thought of fountains and the feeling of a magical, secret place that a garden can give. Martha created a garden that unfurls itself little by little, like a spiral. And, like a magical secret, it is one discovery after another."

The magic begins just inside the front portal. Visitors pass through a wooden gate in a plain brown adobe wall and step down into a world of color and intrigue. The wall along the stairway is hot pink, the railing a deep purple spiral. The other walls shade into luscious pink colors. The ground is covered with gravel, and the whole courtyard is filled with a grid of crab apple trees and square, flat fountains tiled in primary colors. Added to this are colored lights in the fountains. The grid lines turn out to be runnels that channel water from fountain to fountain; like the fountains, the tiles of the runnels sport bright primary hues.

The garden sits right in the landscape, but its paths are obscure. "It is a hidden garden," Dickenson notes. "You come upon it with the fountains and trees, with things growing on the walls. It's very mysterious. You've got to find your way through it. You are forced to figure it out, and it's not too easy."

It is a cloistered garden, a walled oasis, that feels much more intimate than it appears in photographs. In real life, its intimacy is quite spiritual. For some visitors, the spirituality seems to be Zen-like; to others, the effect feels Moorish.

The cloistered main garden is an artwork marked by vibrant color and strong geometries: flat fountains with colored lights at night; long, straight runnels in tiny, colorful tiles; the strong stairway, and white marble boulders around the crab apple trees.

*Opposite, massive
wooden doors from the
parking court open to
reveal the shock of a
hot pink wall.*

*Below, left, containers
help conserve water.
Beside a folk art figure,
a terra-cotta pot is
packed with Japanese
miscanthus grass,
marigolds, lantana, and
purple lobelia. Right, a
folk art cat preens in
proximity to Russian
sage and aspen trees.*

If the courtyard garden has more than one kind of spirituality, it also has a dual personality. By day it seems minimalistic, almost bare. At night, with the fountain lights glowing like exotic jewels, it becomes ethereal.

The cloister of the courtyard spills into a separate, rear garden by way of a stunning staircase with a fantasy mosaic embedded in its adobe wall. The mosaic tells a magical fairy tale that mixes wandering mermaids, seashells, angels, and horses among its many apparitions. Mirrored fragments dot the wall, a nifty trick that gives it a filigreed, see-through appearance, "like Alice through the looking glass. . . . This whole wall reminds me of outsider art, somewhat naive, but unique and beautiful."

In contrast to the enclosed courtyard cloister in front, at its back this garden opens wide to a mountain view as big as all outdoors. "You can't compete with the landscape here," explains Dickenson. "We decided not to try to fight it, but to join it." Above the pool, a bold swath of yuccas holds its own, standing out by virtue of strong shape and regimental arrangement. In keeping with the large scale, oversized containers are arrayed around the pool; they brighten the scene with perennial mixes and topiaries. Still, the rocky New Mexico landscape comes up to the wall, with daisies, penstemon, and other native flowers adding cheerful color and vitality to the dry terrain.

Artworks collected by Dickenson—including sculptures of twigs, breasts, and fans—are placed around the backyard area. Above the pool, the guest-house roof is covered over with bright green grass—a lawn in the heart of the desert. This expanse resembles an abstract canvas, and Dickenson calls it her "Ode to Ohio," in honor of the lawns in her home state. Even the pool presents a picture. A notch has been cut into the adobe wall at the back to open up a mountain view for the contemplative pleasure of swimmers.

While Dickenson's garden is vastly different from the typical garden in Santa Fe (or almost anywhere else for that matter), it really makes a great deal of sense in this climate. The elements that define monumental desert gardens like the Alhambra—protective walls, clean geometry, cooling fountains, and shady trees—also provide inspiration here. This garden in fact has very old roots, recasting the venerable tradition of desert gardens into the realm of the new.

THE ART OF THE GARDEN

The natural landscape comes right up to the garden wall of the pool-side terrace. Dickenson's art collection is consistent with the desert environment. Opposite, a metal sculpture, "Madame Pompadour," by Uruguayan artist Dardo Socas.

At right, Paul Canfield's metal sculpture, "Figure as Landscape," rests on the ground, while Bill Gilbert's twig sculpture reaches skyward.

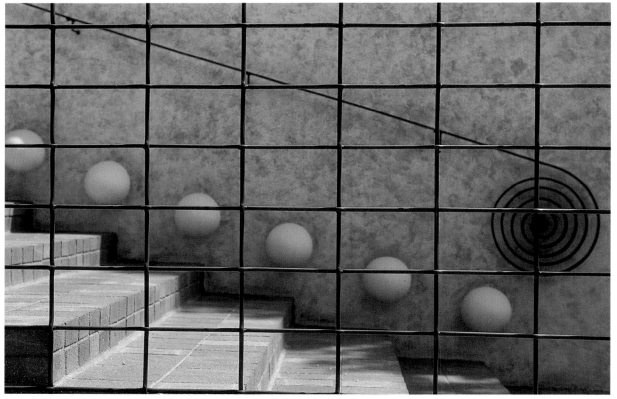

Top, yucca cuts a wide swath above a pink adobe wall and terraces uphill from pool to house. The groundcover is yellow iceplant. Bottom, the spiral, Dickenson's favorite shape, inspired the metal stairway rail.

Opposite, the staircase linking front and rear gardens sports a fantasy-wall mosaic by Lloyd Ortiz, embellished with a personal collection of sea shells, crockery, little figures, and jugs. The mirrored tiles give a lacy, through-the-looking-glass intrigue.

Page 192: A trellis at a fruitstand in the Santa Fe countryside.